SHE CAN
PROSPER

Unlocking financial independence and empowering women to thrive

Diane Watson

Cover image by: Lisa Webb, Pinkfrog
Book design by: SWATT Books Ltd

Printed in the United Kingdom
First printing, 2023

ISBN: 978-1-7384212-0-6 (Paperback)
ISBN: 978-1-7384212-1-3 (eBook)

Diane Watson
Weatherby, West Yorkshire

DEDICATION

This book is dedicated firstly to my parents, Albert and Doris, two inspiring guides who encouraged and taught me how to be a financially secure woman. They showed me the reason why being financially independent opens the door to the freedom to live life on my terms.

Secondly, to my children, Hannah and Luke, who were the reason I chose to follow my dream of running my own business and creating financial prosperity for us all. They are the next generation in my family to be following in my footsteps, creating their own financial futures.

And finally, to Debbie Gilbert. Every little girl wants a sister and I found mine in 2020 when I became a member of Sister Snog, a tribe of remarkable businesswomen. It was there that I was introduced to my Sister, Debbie Gilbert. We have embarked on a journey together and writing this book has been a part of it. I would like to thank Debbie for her encouragement, unbelievable support and wisdom. She has been the driving force who has been instrumental in helping me create the book I always wanted to write.

TESTIMONIALS

"This book is brimming with original content, all aligned to financial freedom. All the messages are supremely relevant, particularly for those who have their life ahead of them." – **HELA WOZNIAK-KAY**

"I loved this book and have found it an invaluable resource. The real-life stories make this relatable and it has spurred me on to book an appointment with a financial advisor. Brilliant content in an easy-to-read format." – **CLARE RUSH**

"What an eye opener! I now have all the information necessary to start planning my financial future. I am only 25 and I hadn't really given much thought to it. But this has made me think and now I will act! The book has been easy to read and understand and has filled in a lot of financial blanks for me." – **JADE SMALL**

CONTENTS

Foreword

Imagine growing up with parents who really understood the value of financial independence, and how this could shape your life.

As the daughter of two financial advisors, personal finances and financial education featured heavily in my life. I didn't realise this wasn't the norm until I reached a certain age and conversed with friends who seemed to know little about pensions, mortgages, life and critical illness cover. I'm now 35, married with a toddler and that knowledge and grounding is even more important.

During my childhood, I never felt that struggle regarding having enough money to live the life I wanted. Whilst I wasn't aware of that then, I can now look back and realise that I was very fortunate.

I always knew our life was very different from my mum's growing up, and a far cry from Nana's childhood. It was as different as day and night. I was educated in a private school and lived in a large house with a beautiful garden. Life was very easy for us. Now, I can appreciate how different their lives were to mine growing up, and the struggles my Nana faced, living in poverty.

I'm grateful for all I have. I have so much admiration for my Nana, and how she turned her life around – her journey was impressive. She is incredibly resilient and was determined to create a better life for herself and her family. It's inspirational to have a woman like that in your life; she never let her gender or social class stand in her way.

This theme continued with my mum, who worked as the breadwinner from when I went to school. This was very different to most of my peer group at a small private school in the 90s. I always felt my mum had a handle on our finances, which was incredibly reassuring.

We had a short period of financial issues when my father lost his job. It was noticeable in terms of the atmosphere at home and gave me an insight into what can happen when something significant happens to disrupt the finances of a family unit, but deep down, I always felt my mum would sort the situation out.

When my parents divorced, I had already left home, but I knew Mum would be fine and would ensure she was in control of her financial future. I know of friends for whom a divorce or death in their family has caused significant worry, and many have had to step in to support their parents, which is a challenging dynamic for the parent–child relationship.

I went to university and then, after my degree, completed an MSc, which led to a good corporate job with a comprehensive package including a pension scheme, family leave policies, as well as healthcare and life insurance.

When I met my husband, we shared the same thoughts and values around money, which was essential to me. We have open conversations about money and a joint bank account, so everything is transparent. We have always shared our expenses, even in the relatively early days, and I value that I don't have to ask permission to spend money even though I earn less than he does.

My mum has always instilled in me the importance of having a will and lasting power of attorney. I speak about this with my friends and remind them how important it is, as you never know what will happen. They probably think I'm a real bore! Often, I find myself in an advisory role with friends' financial problems and questions, perhaps because they know my background.

One of the most important things that my mum has instilled in me is that as a woman, self-sufficiency is essential to get a promising career and have your own money. The main principle she taught me is that you must know how much money you need for the essentials, save some for the future, and then use the money left to enjoy life.

She definitely lives this motto and grabs life with both hands!

I am so proud that my mum was a trailblazer, breaking the ground for other women in the financial services world. Women in this profession were rare when they qualified, and most were not running their own businesses.

Integrity has always been important to her, and she emphasises doing the right thing for her clients, even if this doesn't make her any money. I have seen her spend a lot of time advising my friends and even my friends' friends for nothing. She is incredibly generous with her time.

Her guidance, love and advice have stood me in good stead in life, and I will be passing this wisdom on to my son to ensure he grows up with good values around money. Even though his parents have both been fortunate to have comfortable upbringings, I will ensure he knows where he comes from – especially those strong women who have made it all happen.

I am so pleased she has written this book to share all her knowledge and advice, which I know will benefit many women. This book will help anyone, whatever their background, take control of their financial destiny and make the best decisions to create a solid financial future.

Hannah Watson

INTRODUCTION

Diane Watson – My Story

The aim of this book is to educate and inspire you to take action with regards to your financial affairs. My experience of the financial industry spans over 30 years and I have collated my knowledge and that of other experts to help you understand how to manage your money.

I have also shared the stories of women who have been through financial upheaval or who have created fantastic financial plans which have resulted in some great options for them in their life.

I am fortunate that I grew up with the best female financial role models any child could have. It is a major reason for setting up She Can Prosper and writing this book.

My mother and grandmothers were determined, astute and intelligent women. They recognised that the only people they could rely on in life were themselves. That's why they took control of the family finances and went out to work at a time when half the female population didn't.

I learned from around the age of five that my parents came from impoverished families. Our day-to-day lives taught me much about living within my means and taking responsibility for my present and future.

My mum feared financial shortages, not being able to pay the bills and put food on the table. This drove her to save religiously. She had many savings plans, which sent a powerful message to me, leaving me in no doubt that my future success and financial security were my responsibility and were not to be left to a man. I was taught to budget carefully and live within my means. It worked; I have never had an outstanding balance on a credit card or accumulated any debt apart from a mortgage and a car purchase.

My work ethic was strong; as a teenager, it was babysitting for neighbours, then I worked part-time in retail. When I went to university, my parents were earning too much for me to obtain a grant, so I had to pay my way. My financial education made all the difference. I always lived within my means. That meant I didn't go out every night partying because I couldn't afford it. And to make sure I had enough money to get by every term, I worked every holiday. People ask me if I missed out. I always answer, of course not! It helped me get a good degree and gave me a solid foundation for my financial future.

After I graduated and landed my first job, like my parents I was determined to buy my own house as soon as possible. I earned a small salary but focused on saving as much as possible to get the deposit together. Mum's powerful lessons helped me to climb onto the property ladder before my friends. All it took was a bit of discipline and determination to achieve my goal. I progressed my career, working in sales and then training. I took every opportunity offered to me and trebled my salary after just a few years.

After I got married, I focused on building a savings pot, which meant that when I had children, I could take some time off to raise them. I also put in place life insurance and critical illness cover.

You can see the theme here: **Decide what you want, set a financial goal, focus and reap the rewards.**

After four years as a stay-at-home mum, I needed to return to work to get my brain working again. My husband was a financial advisor, and I had worked extensively with the financial services industry when selling training solutions. It seemed the obvious thing to do. But I wasn't going to work for someone else anymore. So, I began planning my own business, and a year later I had fully qualified as a financial advisor.

From the start, I was determined to be successful; there were few women in financial services and very few graduates, so I was an outlier. I worked hard to build the business and networked like crazy! I created my plan for that first year, knowing I still had money in the bank to support us. My focus was creating strategic partnerships with other companies who referred work to me.

There were moments of doubt about whether running a business was right. We moved house, had a big mortgage, liked good holidays and now had school fees to consider and, of course, I had the costs of the business on top. It could be very daunting if I thought about it too much!

For all the struggles, my grit and drive saw the business start to take off. Being a woman was hard in one way, but in others, it helped. I was different, I could attract female clients, and many law firms liked my approach because it stood out from the crowd. I was seen as a safe pair of hands for the typical female-led disciplines in law – bereavement, serious illness and divorce. I was also passionate about putting the client first and providing holistic planning for all the clients' needs, not just the areas I could help with. There were ups and downs, but when times were difficult, I returned to tight financial budgeting to ensure I kept to the mantra "live within your means". So, for periods, it meant no expensive holidays or other little luxuries.

The business was thriving again when I was hit by the challenge of divorce from my husband. It felt like financial suicide. You go from having money between you to having to split everything, halving each partner's wealth. But it was easier because I had built financial independence and had the resources to leave the marriage. Many women who cannot afford to do so are stuck in unhappy marriages or relationships because their husband or partner controls the purse strings.

I focused on work and what I wanted to achieve. I had moved the business to the St James's Place Partnership, and it was my ambition to become a Principal Partner. To achieve this, I knew I had to work harder. I talked a lot about it. One of my team said to me one day, "What are you doing about it?" She was what everybody needs – someone who keeps you accountable. She made me visualise what that achievement looked like.

I visited Spencer House, originally owned by Princess Diana's ancestor, John 1st Earl Spencer, in the mid-eighteenth century. I had meetings there regularly as it was a key location for the St James's Place Partnership in London. In the entrance hall was a massive open fire. I visualised becoming a Principal Partner; I saw myself in front of that fire, shaking hands with the company's founder Mike Wilson, as he handed me a bottle of champagne. It did drive me on. When I eventually made it, Mike was sadly too ill to come to Spencer House, but he phoned me and arranged a visit to his flat, where the symbolic bottle of champagne was handed over.

Strangely, when I finally achieved this long-dreamt-of goal, I thought, "And?" I didn't feel any different. I was still the driven, hard-working individual who had got to the top of the mountain. Nothing changed.

After 25 years of running my own company, and approaching the age of 60, I decided to sell and merge my business with another. This has given me choices and a more relaxed way of life.

With more time, I gave more thought to my real passion: helping other women. I have wanted to write a book since I was a little girl.

More importantly, I want to inspire women to act so they can build their financial future. From this idea She Can Prosper was born. It's a call to action, a belief in the power of women and their potential to succeed.

I haven't told you my story to show how well I've done. I hope you can see that by living within your means, focusing on important financial goals and finding your own purpose to drive you on, you can transform your life. I have faced significant obstacles, just like everyone else. I didn't start with loads of money. I had nothing when I left university. But anyone can choose to act and achieve what they want.

I've been driven to be the best I can be and achieve as much as possible. I've taken big but educated risks, from relocations to setting up my first business.

You can afford to take risks if you stay informed and remain continually aware of what's going on around you. Without those risks, you'll never achieve your true potential.

I am so glad you have come to this book, and I hope you will find a few ideas that will make a difference in your life.

This is a legacy from my mum, where my passion for helping women to control their own lives came from. With her unswerving guidance and support, I got to where I am today. And if I can help change just a handful of lives, it will all be worthwhile.

As you read this book, make notes, create an action plan – don't just leave it in a drawer! This guide will help you throughout your life and equip you to pass your learnings on to others.

Disclaimer

The information contained in this book does not constitute legal or financial advice and should never be used without first consulting with a financial professional to determine what may be best for your individual needs.

CHAPTER ONE

What Is Prosperity?

"Prosperity is not just about accumulating wealth, but about enriching the spirit and fostering growth in all aspects of life." - Unknown

She Can Prosper[1] is designed to help women achieve prosperity through their own actions. But what does prosperity mean? Like many words, it originates from Latin, in this case *prosperitas*, meaning "favourable state or outcome, success", from which in turn comes *prospserus*, "agreeable to one's wishes, successful".

So, prosperity is not necessarily about having great wealth. Whilst economic success is part of what we think of as prosperity, there are other elements too.

The Collins English Dictionary defines prosperity as: "A successful, flourishing, or thriving condition, especially in financial respects. Good fortune."

If you follow the advice in this book, there is a good chance you'll have opportunities to thrive, to build a path to a better future.

The question is: how do you get your finances to flourish?

---

1. Both this volume and the organisation, "She Can Prosper".

What Does Prosperity Mean Today?

Financial prosperity

This is probably the first thing you think about when considering what prosperity means to you. This book aims to give you the tools and inspiration to achieve financial prosperity for yourself.

But what does it mean?

Financial prosperity is a state where you no longer need to worry about having enough money to pay your bills, to put food on the table, to give your kids a great upbringing and to fulfil your own needs and desires. What that looks like is different for everyone.

The most important thing to keep in mind is that your prosperity is not governed by how much you earn, but how much you save. Remember my story as a young woman out of university in her first job. I was earning just £5,500 a year, but I managed to save £3,000 for a deposit on my first house in just over a year. **Prosperity can be achieved in the long term if you cut your cloth accordingly.**

Personal development

My mum always said the foundation of everything is a good education. You may have been lucky enough to go to a great school, get a good degree and be working in your dream job. Yet for many that's not reality. Too many schools don't deliver the education children need. There are many complex reasons why this is the case, and this is not the place to discuss them.

My point is, in the same way I preach about taking responsibility for our financial future, I also believe in the importance of being educated. Again, this means different things to different people.

But there are some fundamentals:

- Build your knowledge about financial products.
- Learn the essential tax rules.
- Study how to invest, and you'll build your wealth if you create, then follow, a plan.

Learn to communicate as well as you can. Whether sending emails, doing a presentation at work or simply talking to friends and family, the better you communicate, the happier your life will be.

And make sure you have basic numeracy skills. That doesn't mean being a whizz at trigonometry. But practise mental maths and think about how numbers relate to each other. When you apply that to your finances, you'll be amazed how much clearer things are and you'll be able to make good financial decisions.

But there is so much more to becoming a fully rounded person who really can prosper in today's competitive world.

What's most important is that you understand your passions and drivers. Prosperity ultimately means to thrive. Identify your goals and build your knowledge to help you get where you want to be, and you can thrive personally as well as financially.

Helping others

If you're not aware of the health benefits of being kind to others, then trust me, they are real. That's not just my opinion – it comes from a raft of research programmes carried out across the globe. Volunteering, helping an elderly neighbour or just enquiring how a colleague's day is going are all ways to show kindness. And there are numerous benefits:

- You will reduce feelings of isolation, making you feel part of a community.
- Your life will remain in perspective, reducing stress levels.

- It not only improves your mental health, but that of those you help too.
- Your community becomes a happier place. The more acts of kindness people receive, the more they do for others.
- Helping others has been proven to help you live longer. It boosts the immune system, giving more protection against illness.
- Health benefits also include lowering blood pressure, a great way to prevent cardiovascular disease.
- Your self-esteem will be boosted significantly. That in turn will lead to you making better life choices as you value yourself more.

Once again this is about taking responsibility for your actions. The more money you have, the more you can help charities and causes you really care about. But this section is not about the need for money. I can't emphasise enough that true prosperity is as much about who you are in your community as how well you're doing financially.

Emotional well-being

How you feel about yourself is fundamental to every part of the prosperity you create in your life. Many people struggle with low self-esteem, especially women. So, it's vital you create a framework to keep your energy levels high, your mental health at its best and maintain relationships that nourish you.

There are things you must do to ensure those goals are achieved. They include:

- **Schedule time for you.** Whether it's going to the gym, reading a book or just having a hot, relaxing bath, take time to recharge your batteries and reconnect with yourself.
- **Spend time with people that matter.** Arrange regular date nights with your partner. Spend quality time with your kids rather than just ferrying them from one activity to another. Make time to call or see friends. Remember how important your parents are, if you are lucky enough to still have them in your lives. These relationships underpin your life and, in truth, most of us are guilty of under-investing in them.

- **Take a break.** Whether it's a big family holiday, a city break or an activity weekend, break up the routine, do what you love and boost your mental health.
- **Write a journal every day.** Think about what you're grateful for. What are your daily goals, how did you do yesterday? Note what made you feel angry, happy, curious. Research shows that journalling is as effective as cognitive behavioural therapy at preventing depression and reducing stress.
- **Exercise.** Whether you're a gym junkie or you prefer to go for a walk, move your body and get your heart beating a bit faster. The benefits of that oxygen getting to your brain and the strengthening of your heart will make a difference to you mentally and physically.

As you can see, prosperity is a multi-faceted concept that needs investment by you in every area of life to ensure you achieve it. Each is interconnected. Those with poor mental health often find it difficult to focus on financial issues.

If you're unaware of how to build your financial security and what's happening in the markets, you won't be able to make informed decisions about the best strategy for you. Suffer from poor physical health and you may struggle to work. That means less income.

Ultimately, whilst this book is aimed at helping you take control of your financial security, please remember that taking responsibility for everything that influences your ability to do that is just as important.

The Four Life Stages of Prosperity – Your 20s, 30s, 40s and 50s

Not everyone gets that great financial start in life. Being given a trust fund at 18 is rare. Once they leave school, most people are faced with grasping their financial future and learning how to create the best life they can.

It is typical for a teenager to take the view that life is for living, not worrying about the future. But to enjoy a long and happy life, it's important to consider what you can do to create the best possible financial security.

For each decade of your life, there are things you need to consider, which will change with life events such as getting married or having children. This book includes lists for each decade.

Take some time to run through the checklist for your decade. You will find more detailed explanations and advice in this book to help you understand where you need to act. Remember, it's essential to consult with a financial advisor to tailor these considerations to your specific circumstances and financial goals.

Twenties

In your 20s, it's a great time to start laying the foundation for a solid financial future.

Here is a checklist of important things to consider.

- [ ] **Build an emergency fund.** Your fund is there to cover unexpected expenses, for example, a car breakdown. Aim to keep three to six months' worth of living expenses.

- [ ] **Pay off debt.** If you have loans or credit card debt, focus on paying off the highest interest balances first. Minimise debt as much as possible to avoid paying excessive interest over time.

- [ ] **Start investing for retirement. By doing it now, you will build more future wealth.** Get advice to get ahead and create a sizeable pension fund. The earlier you start, the less you need to save each month.

- [ ] **Set a budget.** Establish a budget to track your income and expenses. Learn to live within your means, save more and avoid unnecessary debt. Your bank will almost certainly have an app to help you easily track your spending (see Chapter 2).

☐ **Save for life goals.** Whether it's a deposit for a house, a dream holiday or purchasing a car, create a savings plan. Set up separate savings accounts for each goal and contribute regularly.

☐ **Invest in yourself.** Consider investing in your education or skills development. This could involve taking courses, attending workshops or conferences, or acquiring certifications that can enhance your career prospects and earning potential.

☐ **Start building credit.** Open a credit card and use it responsibly to start building your credit history. Pay your bills on time and keep your credit utilisation low. A good credit score will benefit you when applying for loans or getting a mortgage.

☐ **Start a side hustle.** Explore opportunities to generate additional income through a side hustle. It can help you save more, pay off debt faster or invest in your goals. What skills do you have? You can do additional work online, so investigate the options.

☐ **Develop good financial habits.** Cultivate good money management habits such as tracking expenses, avoiding impulsive purchases and practising delayed gratification. These habits will serve you well throughout your life.

☐ **Plan for the unexpected.** Consider getting insurance, such as critical illness or income protection insurance, to protect yourself from unforeseen circumstances that could disrupt your financial stability.

You might feel overwhelmed reading this list. However, it's not that difficult to put these measures into place.

OUR SURVEY

She Can Prosper surveyed a group of 100 women aged 18–30 to gain insight into their money mindset and financial plans. Here is a summary of the results.

Are you more proactive or reactive when it comes to financial decisions?

Just over 50 per cent felt they were more reactive when making financial decisions; 20 per cent shared they were both reactive and proactive!

> *"A little bit of both, proactive in paying my bills and saving first, but reactive because I sometimes dip into them for treats."*

What are your short-term financial goals?

The number one financial goal was buying a property, followed by saving and investing. A small percentage were keen to clear their debts. Around 10 per cent of our respondents were saving to travel.

Are you actively saving for your long-term financial security, such as retirement or buying a home? If yes, what strategies are you using?

It was great to see that 80 per cent of our respondents already have pensions and long-term savings plans. One of our respondents was paying additional contributions to her pension, taking advantage of the fact that her company would match it.

> *"I had previously made some investments which contribute to retirement planning, and I contribute to my pension every month at the highest percentage that my organisation matches. I have bought a home and rent one of the rooms, contributing to the mortgage and upkeep."*

What resources or tools do you use to effectively track your expenses and budget?

The Excel spreadsheet was the most popular choice for tracking expenditures, followed by Fudget, Monzo and Emma. Some respondents were tracking through their banking app.

How do you handle debt, such as student loans or credit card balances? Are you actively working towards paying them off?

Around 70 per cent of respondents are paying off student loans, and a small percentage, around 5 per cent, have no debt. Twenty-five per cent were paying their debts each month, with 2 per cent of those clearing their balance each month.

How do you balance spending on personal experiences and indulgences with saving for future financial stability?

Many of our respondents cited that searching for deals and discounts was a priority. Some have found it useful to have separate savings accounts along with planning their budget.

> *"I am realistic when dividing savings and spending money and using my spending money for hobbies or nights out rather than the newest clothes or technology."*

Balancing saving with spending was a challenge for some:

> *"With difficulty! It's a fine line between being young/ living in the now and not saying 'no' to a night out or weekend away because the money might be put to better use within a house deposit (or similar). This has only been made harder with the cost-of-living crisis. Young people still want to play young, but we have to sacrifice something to do so, social life or future savings."*

"I rarely hold back on taking an opportunity for a personal experience over savings, as I believe we work hard and deserve to enjoy the money we make. However, I like to save a minimum of £1,000 a year, so if I see that I'm not on track for this, I will assess and save more the following month."

Do you feel confident discussing financial matters with others, such as friends, family or financial advisors? If not, what barriers do you face?
It was great to read that 97 per cent of our respondents felt they had people to turn to, and many had also started using a financial advisor.

Some respondents felt uncomfortable talking to people about money, but others considered taking advice, realising this was the best course of action.

What role does financial education play in your life? Have you sought out resources to improve your financial knowledge, and if so, what?
A small percentage, 6 per cent, had actively tried to improve their financial knowledge. Martin Lewis, Money Supermarket and Denise Duffield-Thomas, along with family and friends, were mentioned as information sources.

Our survey revealed that a high proportion of young women were on track. The areas of balancing savings with spending and retirement plans were the areas that needed more thought and attention.

Read through these questions yourself and see where you sit in terms of your actions regarding your finances. Then use this book to increase your knowledge.

CREATING A FINANCIAL FUTURE IN YOUR TWENTIES

Abby's story

Abby is in her 20s and is an ambitious young financial advisor who has recognised that securing your future means making good decisions today. She is an excellent example of a young woman who has learnt the lessons of financial prudence and has set goals she is focused on achieving.

Abby recently qualified as a financial adviser at a leading wealth management firm. At 28, she is on track to build financial security, save the money she needs to buy a house, and start a career that could set her up for life.

Abby's background

Abby came from a family that instilled a work ethic in her from a young age. Her dad was a full-time financial advisor who worked hard to make sure he could provide for his family. Abby started working at 16 and was taught to put away a percentage of her earnings and how to budget, assigning fixed costs and discretionary spending into different pots.

Her parents set boundaries, so she did not rely on them for everything. "I knew early on in life what I could spend at any time and the value of money," said Abby.

Abby trained in marketing and started in a PR and marketing role with a small charity. While she enjoyed her work, she realised that development options were few and a long-term career in the sector was limited. She had built enough savings to take time to consider what to do next.

"I spoke to my parents and consulted my network, including Diane, who we had known for years," recalled Abby. She wanted to be self-employed and had to follow a path that would build financial security. Making her own money was a huge driver. Diane suggested training as a financial advisor, like her and her dad. An opportunity had come up with a major player, and Abby grasped it.

Abby has been working hard to get her qualifications. Learning about the varied financial products in her portfolio has made her realise even more the need for careful financial planning and making good decisions. "Once I am qualified, I'll set up a personal pension to monitor and track myself. I will have the advantage of greater knowledge and support from experts around me."

Other assets are already in place. "I have workplace pensions that are appreciating and a Help-to-buy ISA[2] that I may convert into a Lifetime ISA."

With all exams now completed, she will soon be able to build her career. She plans to invest in marketing to generate leads and create a networking strategy to meet potential clients and introducers.

Abby wanted to be self-employed, so she was in control of her financial future. She doesn't want to answer to anyone else, justifying why she should earn more. "I don't want to wait for annual reviews to get a pay rise. If I work hard, I can earn more. I don't want a ceiling put on me."

Creating financial balance

Abby has a wide friendship group who, like her, are in their 20s. Unlike her, most save little, following the philosophy of "live for today". She hears it everywhere: "There is a strong narrative among my peers that nobody knows what will happen in the future. As we only live once, we must live for the moment." That drives needless spending and a distinct lack of saving.

She bemoans the high levels of consumerism many of her friends display: "They spend heavily online. They often buy new clothes, a new bag, or just overspend when they go out. My mentality is much more prudent, especially as I get close to qualifying as a financial advisor."

---

2. An ISA is an Individual Savings Account in the UK which allows tax-efficient saving.

Having attended private school, many of her friends come from similar backgrounds. She admits that leads to complacency. "I have friends who were put through private school, have been given or promised large sums of money, and, at present, believe they don't need to worry too much. That means they spend beyond their means and dip into their savings because they know they can lean on their parents." But Abby knows that things can change and that an endless supply in life is never guaranteed. That's why she advocates a more responsible approach. "I recognise I must take control of my finances. My grandmother was a saver, and so was my mother. It's given me a similar attitude."

Financial goals

Abby intends to work hard to achieve high earnings. But she has one clear priority – to buy her first house. She is currently renting and knows she will need to continue saving to get the deposit she requires, but this seems well within her grasp.

Abby is also putting in place critical illness cover and will take out life insurance once she gets a mortgage. She believes in living within her means – her credit card gets paid off every month: "I only have one to ensure I have a good credit score. I certainly don't use it for everything."

Her view is that people's relationships with money are often based on what they are taught as a child. "I think if you see parents who don't just spend, spend, spend, but put money away, you follow the same path. If your experience is the opposite, or you come from a home lacking money, it often leads to overspending as an adult."

Abby's advice to young people

Having become increasingly aware of the need to plan towards financial security, Abby thinks young people need to move away from current mindsets. "I would say, try not to follow the advice that we should all live for today. I'm not saying we shouldn't enjoy our lives, but we should have more concern about what will happen in the future. Thinking your parents will always come to the rescue is a dangerous strategy."

Abby supports saving from a young age: "Saving young can make an enormous difference across your lifetime. Given our life expectancy is increasing, it's a vital consideration. You don't want to miss the opportunity to enjoy your later years that you worked so hard for."

Her advice is to take a balanced approach. Of course, everyone should be doing fun stuff in their lives, but they need to keep a close eye on their future too.

Thirties

In your 30s, building a solid financial foundation and setting yourself up for long-term financial success is essential.

Here is a checklist of financial goals you should consider implementing during this decade:

- [ ] **Emergency fund.** It is crucial to save three to six months' living expenses in a readily accessible account. This fund acts as a safety net in case of unexpected events.

- [ ] **Debt repayment.** Prioritise paying off high-interest debt, such as credit card debt or loans.

- [ ] **Retirement savings.** If you still need to start a pension plan, do it now!

- [ ] **Housing.** Work towards buying your own home. If you still need to do this, prioritise in this decade!

- [ ] **Investing and saving.** If you have a pension and have purchased your first home, consider investing and saving. Seek professional advice to understand different investment options and create a balanced strategy.

☐ **Career advancement.** Focus on advancing your career and increasing your earning potential. Invest in professional development, additional certifications or courses to enhance your skills and qualifications.

☐ **Insurance cover.** Review your insurance needs and ensure adequate cover for life, critical illness and income protection. This is especially important if you have dependants. Consider private health care, especially if you work for yourself. NHS waiting times can be very long, so you can get treatment faster and return to work quicker.

☐ **Estate planning.** Get a will in place and powers of attorney. Although it may seem early, having a will ensures your assets are distributed according to your wishes and protects your loved ones.

☐ **Financial education.** Continuously educate yourself about personal finance. Read books, listen to podcasts and consult a financial advisor to enhance your knowledge and make informed financial decisions. There is a useful list of resources at the end of this book.

☐ **Strive for balance.** You can enjoy your life today and save for the future. Allocate funds for experiences and things that bring you joy in the present.

DEALING WITH UNEXPECTED EVENTS IN YOUR THIRTIES

Clare's story

You can never predict what may happen to you and when. All you can do is prepare for every eventuality. Clare's story illustrates why financial protection is a must, even if you are a fit and healthy woman in your 30s.

No woman thinks they are going to get breast cancer aged 33. But that was the fate that befell Clare nine years ago.

She was a young woman facing a hugely challenging battle with cancer that continued to impact her life for several years. However, working for an employer who provided excellent financial protection and private medical insurance gave her the tools to deal with the fallout.

Being diagnosed with breast cancer

Clare had built a successful career in banking. Like many women, she tended to put other people first. Looking after her own health was not the priority it should have been. However, when she started to notice intense pain in her breast, she knew she should get tested.

Clare was diagnosed with breast cancer and had to undergo a lumpectomy, chemotherapy and radiotherapy. After months of sapping treatment, Clare was given a good prognosis. She was relieved to know she was cancer-free, but it was the start of a major period of change for Clare.

"A lot changed in my life as I started to deal with my cancer. My marriage was breaking down, and my life-threatening situation made me review everything," she explained.

Critical illness cover makes a difference

With so much happening in her life, Clare hadn't really considered her financial options. By chance, an employee flexible benefits statement came through the post. Reading its contents, she realised she had critical illness cover as part of her package. "I wasn't sure if I should ring up about my cover. I felt a bit of a fraud as my cancer wasn't terminal," said Clare.

But she wasn't a fraud. When she declared her triple negative breast cancer diagnosis, an aggressive form, she received a cheque for a significant sum a week later. "It lifted a huge weight from my shoulders," she said. As Clare says, the rest of life's stresses don't disappear just because you have cancer. Thankfully, critical illness was able to make a real difference to her quality of life.

Why private medical insurance was so important

Whilst critical illness had been essential in helping Clare move forward in her life, private medical insurance was an equally important benefit, as it speeded up her treatment. It also made her more comfortable. For example, Clare was able to have chemotherapy treatments at home.

But the story does not stop with her successful cancer treatment. Four years later, she returned for an oncology consultation. Having cancer so young is unusual and is often linked to genetic mutations. The BRCA1 and BRCA2 genetic mutations have been identified as major causes of hereditary cancer, together with other mutations. Around 1 in 400 people have this mutation and it affects men as well as women. Clare tested positive for the BRCA1 mutation, despite having no family history of cancer. The discovery had serious implications for the probability of a recurrence: "My oncologist told me I had about an 80 per cent chance of further breast cancer and a 70 per cent probability of developing ovarian cancer."

The oncologist strongly recommended she have a full hysterectomy and double mastectomy. The odds were so high she simply couldn't take the chance of letting nature take its course. These surgeries were classed as "preventative", despite the fact she was already a cancer survivor, which would have meant a wait time of eighteen months to two years. Once again, private medical insurance made the difference, and she was lucky enough to have both operations within three months.

Her cover not only allowed her quicker treatment, but it also meant she returned to work earlier, a benefit for her and her employer.

The impact of surviving cancer

Having come through her breast cancer and dealt with two major operations to protect against a reoccurrence, Clare was ready to change her life completely. In 2022 she gave up her job in banking after over 20 years helping SMEs,[3] corporates and working in major operations.

"I wanted to do something different, and I was lucky to be given an opportunity, which allowed me to set up my own company, Leading Operations. I now help businesses improve performance and scale for growth as an independent advisor," said Clare.

She describes how her cancer journey changed her: "It makes you re-evaluate everything, your relationships, your job, your life. It really was a positive thing for me because I wouldn't be where I am today without my cancer diagnosis."

She is testament to the fact that cancer does not need to be an end, it can truly be a new beginning.

She has also ensured she continues to invest in every form of financial protection now that she no longer enjoys the bank's benefits package.

Clare's advice to young women

When you're young, you may well think serious illnesses like cancer won't happen to you – especially with no family history. Clare looks back now and

---

3. SMEs are small and medium-sized enterprises.

realises how much she put others first. "My advice to my younger self would be, 'spend less time focusing on work and everyone else, and take more time to focus on your own needs and well-being'." Those needs include nutrition, exercise, health screening and finances.

She has experienced first-hand the importance of critical illness cover and private medical insurance and advises all women to put those protections in place no matter their age, if they can afford it.

Clare advises: "Even as a young woman, review where your finances are. What do you have in place? Where are the gaps and what are they? Speak to an advisor about putting the right protection in place."

Forties

Financial considerations in your 40s can be crucial. Many people at this stage of life will have others that are dependent on them. Your life may now encompass additional responsibilities, dependent children and a mortgage.

Here are the fundamental financial considerations you need to be aware of:

- ☐ **Retirement planning.** This is the time to evaluate your retirement goals and ensure you're on track. Consider increasing your retirement contributions. Work with a financial advisor who can help you create your future financial plans.

- ☐ **Debt management.** If you still have debt, make paying it off a priority and make a promise to yourself not to increase it! Live within your means and save for larger purchases.

- ☐ **Emergency fund.** Ensure you always have an emergency fund of 3–6 months of income.

☐ **Insurance.** Review your insurance policies to ensure adequate coverage for your family's needs. This includes life insurance, critical illness coverage and income protection. You should also investigate private medical cover if you haven't got cover through your work.

☐ **Estate planning.** This is now an urgent task! Make a will and put lasting powers of attorney in place. Dying without a will creates problems for your family, and your estate will follow the rules of intestacy, so it may not go to the people you want to benefit.

☐ **Savings and investments.** Continue to save and invest, as this will give you an excellent foundation for that final stage of your life when you might work less and want to spend time doing the things you love. You might have also inherited money, so work with a financial advisor on the best way to maximise this.

DEALING WITH DEBT IN YOUR FORTIES

Annie's story

Annie's story is a warning to all women about the dangers of spending beyond your means. She got into serious debt, using credit to fuel her spending habit. Here is her story.

My debt just crept up on me. It all began when I got my first job; I was 18 and was out shopping for clothes. When I took my large haul to the counter to pay, the shop assistant offered me a store card and explained that I would get a discount on my purchases if I signed up. I agreed as I didn't really understand what I was signing up for, and it felt like free money. I had the money to buy the clothes but didn't use it. I spent it on other things and paid off just the minimum amount the next month. It seemed an easy way to get what I wanted.

Before long, I had three store cards, three credit cards and a mobile phone contract. I then passed my driving test, immediately got a car loan, and bought my first car, which was way beyond my means. I started taking foreign holidays, and if I couldn't afford it, I just paid for it on my credit card.

As the balances crept up, they increased my limit. My overdraft followed the same path. It kept being extended.

I went on to buy my first house with my first husband with a mortgage deal at the time, which was 105 per cent. This meant I didn't need a deposit. I furnished my new home with furniture on "Buy Now Pay Later" interest-free deals, and without realising it, I was getting further into debt. I made the monthly payments, so to me, there was no problem.

My career progressed, and my salary increased. So, what I owed was never really a consideration. But that all changed when I had two significant life events in succession. I had to take time off sick from work, and my marriage broke down.

When my husband left, I continued to pay the bills and mortgage; he hadn't been great with money and often gambled, so it was a relief that my money was now mine. I removed him from the current account. Then I had a car accident resulting in spinal surgery. It led to eight months off work just after my 40th birthday. Now, my life began to collapse financially.

My company only paid three months on full pay. So, when that expired, I received statutory sick pay, about £100 a week.

My outgoings, including mortgage, bills and debts, were £2,000 a month. My take-home pay was around £3,000 a month, so receiving statutory sick pay meant things started to get into a mess. I had no emergency fund. I wasn't well and didn't contact any of the lenders. I thought I would be off for another month, so I delayed acting. It turned into five more months, and I buried my head in the sand. Default notices started arriving. My bank stopped making payments as I had exceeded my overdraft and stopped my debit and credit cards. I literally had no money.

It was then that I started to act. To begin with, I needed to figure out where to turn. I sat and opened all the letters and realised I was in a terrible financial state. I confided in a friend who suggested I speak to the Citizens Advice Bureau. They were brilliant, and when we totalled my debts, it was almost £26,000. This excluded the mortgage and car loan. The advisor helped me formulate a payment plan for each lender, and we wrote to each one. They all accepted payment plans, and some froze the interest.

I cut up my cards, taking almost five years to clear my debts. Life in my 40s was not how I imagined it. But I knew I had to get things under control. I am now almost 50 and don't owe anyone anything besides my mortgage and car.

But it's been tough, and my biggest lesson to share is don't get into the mess I did. Things happen in life, and the more debt you are in, the harder it is when life throws you a curveball. Don't ever think challenges won't happen to you. Some of my friends are still in debt; their attitude is they deserve the holidays and expensive dresses. So, they use their credit cards. I worry about them and what might happen if they get sick or lose their job.

Annie's advice for young women

My message is simple – don't buy anything on credit unless you plan to clear it when the statement comes in. You have no control if you use credit to purchase things. If the money isn't there, I cannot have it. I now save first, buy later. I learnt a harsh lesson in life and will never repeat that pattern. Getting into debt is so easy and getting out is extremely hard.

Fifties

In your 50s, retirement is becoming a more imminent consideration. During this phase of your life, it's essential to evaluate and adjust your financial plans to ensure a secure future. It's never too late to start savings plans or work on your financial future.

Here are some financial considerations to keep in mind in your 50s.

- **Retirement savings.** Evaluate your retirement savings and make any necessary adjustments. Maximise contributions to your pension and ensure your state pension is up to date. Evaluate your projected income sources during retirement, such as private and state pensions and investment income. Determine if you're on track to meet your retirement income goals and make adjustments if necessary.

- **Investments.** Review your investment portfolio and consider adjusting the allocation to align with your retirement goals and risk tolerance. As you near retirement, you may want to gradually shift towards a more conservative investment approach to protect your savings.

- **Estate planning.** Update your will, establish a power of attorney and consider creating a trust if necessary. This is vital if you have divorced, remarried and have children from a previous marriage. By creating a trust, you can ring-fence their inheritance.

REAPING FINANCIAL BENEFITS IN YOUR FIFTIES

Helen's story

Helen took financial responsibility from a young age and is now, in her 50s, reaping the benefits.

As a child growing up in Stockport, Helen enjoyed sorting items into categories and remembers helping to count the weekly church collection money. This early exposure to coins helped Helen and her sisters foster a savings habit. Helen's younger sister loved saving penny after penny in her NatWest piggy banks. From such beginnings developed a mindset that allowed Helen to retire at 55.

Her story is an excellent example to all women. Being in control of your finances, living within your means and having clear financial goals provides true financial security and leads on to a very comfortable retirement.

Helen's background

Helen came from a happy home. Her parents instilled strong moral and financial values in all four of their daughters. Her father was an accountant with a sense of order. Her mother began her career as a nurse and, as Helen says, was the most positive of role models. Here was a woman who wanted to work and developed herself to the point that she took two masters degrees as a mature student, the second in computing. Towards the end of her career, she became Head of Information and Computation for a major northern teaching hospital with a team of 50 people. She was always humble and very kind, yet highly competent.

Helen's parents loved their children and were generous towards them. But they also ensured the girls did not get the things they wanted without working for them. When Helen's older sister wanted a stereo, she had to earn the money to pay for it by washing dishes at a local hospital throughout her summer holidays.

Helen went to Newcastle University to study Naval Architecture (engineering for shipbuilding), a subject dominated by men. But this was a girl who had been allowed to feel secure in doing things others wouldn't necessarily do and the environment supported and welcomed her. She came out with a 2:1 degree and met the man she married.

Working in a male-dominated environment

After university Helen searched for a role in the shipping industry. Unfortunately, unlike university, she found the male-dominated industry was very uncomfortable with the idea of a woman being equal. Fighting this sexist work environment was not for her. Friends were going into accountancy, the profession her father had been in for years. At that time, attitude was more important for the big accountancy firms than a degree in a specific discipline. It made absolute sense to follow in her father's footsteps.

A big life change

In their 20s the couple led a good life in London. Helen was getting plenty of training in her chosen field, and with two good incomes and no children, they were free to socialise and travel. As the couple approached their 30s, it became apparent they were on different paths. They drifted apart and divorced. This was Helen's first real challenge in making longer-term financial decisions. In splitting their financial assets including property, they had to take into consideration that Helen's husband had not paid into a pension, whilst she had contributed to her defined benefit company pension scheme as soon as she began working. As a result, they had to agree an amount of money to compensate him for his lack of pension contributions as well as trying to balance the difference in their earnings. Both bought other properties and went their separate ways.

Reevaluating financial goals

As she readjusted to a single life, Helen realised she was spending money needlessly. She reviewed her situation and decided there were better things she could do with her money. Helen explained: "I was overspending on frivolous things. I started to think that overpaying the mortgage made more sense. Then I increased my pension contributions. I was lucky to get a job at a large US firm with a defined benefit pension scheme. That was rare by then but very cool! Every time I received a pay rise, I increased contributions towards my pension."

When she turned 40, Helen's thoughts focused on retirement. She had never considered when she would like to stop working. After consideration, she thought 52 was an ideal age – young enough to still take on the physical challenges she enjoyed. The goal had been set, but things changed again when she decided to leave London.

Taking advice from a financial advisor

In her mid-40s, Helen decided she'd had enough of living in the capital. So, she had to decide: did she keep the London property and rent it out, or sell it? She decided to sell.

Helen moved north, which is where she met Diane. "I was trying to get work as a portfolio Finance Director. I met Diane through networking and just thought she really knew what she was talking about."

Helen enlisted Diane to help her optimise her pensions and savings as she approached her 50s. They regularly review how money is apportioned to mortgage overpayments, her pension pot and ISAs.

Not surprisingly, Helen has kept her defined benefit scheme pensions, given the incomes they are projected to produce. Diane has helped her consolidate her other pensions into one pot. And following this approach so assiduously has allowed her to achieve one of her key goals.

The financial planning pays off!

In June 2022, Helen quit work. She had good pensions and money saved in ISAs. She had two items she wanted to pay off. One was the balance on her mortgage, which was only £20,000 by now. The other, a £20,000 car loan.

She had the ability to draw down the money to do both. But being financially savvy, she looked at the impact of taking £20,000 out of her pension against asking her mother for the money. This is not quite as mercenary as it may sound. Her mum was 84 and sitting on healthy savings. Asking her for what was, in effect, an advance on her inheritance, made more sense than taking a lump out of the pension. The money could be paid back if necessary in the future and the transaction was completely transparent to the family; her sisters were fully aware and supportive of the decision.

Helen is enjoying life at a time when many are still thinking about another decade in employment.

And she is working, although it feels like a hobby. Helen is a keen gardener, so a local elderly couple asked her to look after their garden. Their niece followed suit. Now she is earning a reasonable income doing something she loves while having access to savings, using her pensions to absorb her annual tax personal allowance, and having the security of defined pension schemes to draw down in years to come. Life is good.

The bucket list!

Helen is looking forward to an active and fulfilling retirement. Aside from her gardening, Helen is learning tennis and French and is a keen traveller, boosted by visiting friends across Britain and Europe. But she is not leaving her retirement to chance. Helen is a planner and organiser and wrote down everything she wanted to do.

The bucket list was organised into activities that required her to be physically fit, ones that needed more money than others and so on. She then broke them down into the short, medium and long term.

Planning your goals is an excellent way of achieving them. Helen has done that with her finances and will undoubtedly do so with her retirement dreams.

She says of her objectives: "I'm risk averse. I have my list, and I know what I want to do. But if something is costly and I want it enough, I'd return to work."

How it feels to retire early

Helen retired knowing she could afford to live without skimping unnecessarily. But she also knew she couldn't live a life of luxury. She breaks her spending down as follows: "I have basic living expenses, nice-to-haves and completely discretionary spending. The latter includes things like David Lloyd Health Club and my holidays." The holidays are her biggest discretionary spend: "I'm not bothered about clothes or eating out," she says.

She knows she can always cut back on that discretionary spending if she needs to. But travel is a big part of her life these days. She has visited friends in London, Scotland and Norway in the last 12 months and is planning a big trip to the US.

Knowing where her money goes every month means she stays within her means and lives the life she wants to live.

Helen's advice to young women

Helen looks back at her adult life and sees three major trigger points:

- Divorce in her early 30s
- Planning retirement when she hit 40
- Moving away from London in her mid-40s.

That made her reflect: "In my 20s and 30s, I only thought about money for the short term. Looking back, I would have planned my short-, medium- and long-term needs better. That way, you can be clear on what you want at different points in your life and have enough to fall back on when difficult circumstances arise."

Helen's story is about a woman who took control of her finances very young and has achieved much of what she wanted to do in life.

"Developing a good career, saving for the future and setting goals is important. It's the only way to ensure a good life through retirement."

From Poverty to Prosperity

To finish this chapter, I felt it was important to share my mum's story. She demonstrates that you can climb out of abject poverty and, by gaining an education, you can change your fortunes.

The story of Doris Yeamans – my mum and financial role-model

My mother, Doris Yeamans, is a force of nature, never one to moan about the circumstances she found herself in. Her belief is that you are responsible for every element of your life.

Born in 1932, she was the eldest of nine children. Her mother was just 16 when she was born. By the time my mum was five, she had four siblings and was expected to help look after them. Life was tough. Her parents were very poor; she never had new clothes, she had to share a bed with her sister, and meals were often taken in the soup kitchens of Liverpool. In the Second World War, the family endured the Blitz because her mother refused to evacuate them. So her early life was incredibly challenging in many respects.

Mum was a reader and dreamed of going to university. Being so bright and diligent, she was Head Girl at school. Unfortunately, the family was too poor, and she needed to work when she left school to provide income for them. She was offered a place to study to be an Air Traffic Controller, but this meant moving away. It wasn't an option while her family needed her income and support to care for her siblings. She compromised her dreams for the needs of her family. University could not be on the agenda.

When she was 20, she met my dad. He shared the impoverished background she had experienced. His father tragically died when he was just nine. From then on, it was his mission to provide for his mum and younger brother. So, their early struggles mirrored each other, proving to be the catalyst to drive them forwards to a better life.

My mum was determined they would buy a house. Remember, this was post-war Britain, a time when most women were housewives. Women did not generally think about financial issues. However, to get a house, you needed a 50 per cent deposit, out of reach for most people. So, my mum worked two jobs and saved. She had a goal and was driven to achieve it.

My father's work became irregular, also affected by the industrial disputes of that time. My mum couldn't accept that as a sensible way to live, knowing she couldn't guarantee her husband would be able to earn what the family needed.

She decided to go to night school and, over two years, achieved a qualification that enabled her to enrol in a teacher training college to qualify as a teacher. This was in the mid-60s when feminism was starting to awaken, but nearly half the female workforce still stayed at home. Qualifying took real commitment – a 60-mile round trip every day and much additional work to ensure she was ready to enter the classroom.

Mum made a brilliant teacher, and in the early 1970s, she became a head teacher, a deserved reward for all the effort she put into maximising her undoubted talent as a teacher.

Mum had a strong role-model herself. My grandmother was still working as a lollipop lady until her 70th birthday to keep the money rolling in, and she, too, lived within her means. My grandfather had retired, first as a merchant seaman and then as a dock worker, and she too felt the importance of providing for her family.

She became ill shortly after her 70th birthday and was admitted to hospital. One of her requests to my grandad was that when he visited her, he had to bring her carrier bag full of things of importance to her. They had been burgled several times, and she did not want to leave anything to chance. This bag went everywhere with her. Imagine the shock we all had when she died and, in the carrier bag, was an amount of cash equivalent to £25,000 – a vast sum. We can only assume that she had inherited this at some point in her life and felt the best thing to do was to keep it with her. It was such a shame. If she had invested that money, it would have enabled her to buy a house and live a much more comfortable life.

I was so blessed that my mum and grandmother showed me what taking responsibility for yourself looks like. They both believed you must control your destiny and do whatever is necessary to create a stable income.

I noticed with my mum that during her career, she gravitated towards those pupils who were less fortunate than others. She aimed to instil in them the work ethic she had herself. She always encouraged them and ensured they understood that a good education would set them on the right path towards financial security.

When I recollect my childhood, I think of my parents' efforts to enable us to be financially secure. They saved, did not squander their hard-earned income, and lived within their means. Credit was something they did not believe in. The message was that if you couldn't pay for something, you shouldn't put it "on tick", the term for credit back then.

They were confident that they had created a stable financial future for us all, something they had never had in their early years.

One typical example arose when my mother learned that my father would not be entitled to a full widower's pension, even though a male teacher could leave a pension to his widow. So, she acted and put in place a life insurance policy meaning if she died before my dad, he would have a lump sum to help him maintain his lifestyle once her pension had reduced.

Reflecting on my financial journey, I can see how invaluable those messages were to me as a child. They helped me recognise the need to prioritise my financial security. There is a lesson in their story we can all heed. Taking control of your finances is possible and is something all women should aspire to do. It's a vital life skill that will ensure that the life you lead comes with choices.

POINTS FOR PROSPERITY

Define what prosperity means to you.

_____

_____

_____

_____

Where are the gaps from your decade checklist?

_____

_____

_____

_____

What are your top 3 priorities?

1. _____

2. _____

3. _____

CHAPTER TWO

The Four Steps to Building Prosperity

"Prosperity is the outcome of dedication, hard work, and an unwavering belief in oneself." - Marie Curie

f you are going to create financial independence, you must build prosperity to achieve your goal. This chapter offers a practical approach to the four steps I believe you must take to get there. Budgeting will get you on track. How you manage your expenditure against the income you receive determines how much you can save, and helps you work towards a life free of debt.

You may not have considered the importance of your credit score. Yet this is how the financial world sees you as a financially viable individual. Having the best possible score will have a positive impact on the credit cards you can apply for, the loans you can get and the interest you pay. Read on to find out how to maximise your score.

Savings and investments will be a constant theme. This section will help you understand your options in more detail and what you should be doing throughout your life.

Finally, I will help you comprehend the world of pensions more clearly. Your pension is the bedrock of your retirement planning: it is essential you start early, know how much to save and can optimise your returns.

Budgeting

Creating a financial budget is an essential step in managing your money effectively. It helps you track your income and expenses, prioritise your spending and work towards your financial goals.

Without budgeting it can be hard to understand where your money is going. Spending without considering where your money is going won't help you achieve financial security.

If you're a spender and have never created a budget, take time to do a review.

You can learn a lot from looking at your spending habits and working out what is essential and what is waste.

Here's a step-by-step guide to creating a financial budget:

1. **Set your goals.** Start by identifying your financial goals. Do you want to:
   - Pay off debt?
   - Save for a house?
   - Save for a holiday?
   - Buy a car?
   - Build an emergency fund?

   Having clear goals will help you prioritise your spending and make informed decisions.

2. **Calculate your income.** Determine your total monthly income from all sources. Include your salary, side hustles, rental income and any other sources of revenue.

3. **Track your expenses.** Review your bank statements, credit card bills and receipts to track your expenses over the past few months. Categorise your expenses into different groups and differentiate between fixed expenses (those that remain the same each month, such as rent/mortgage, loan payments) and variable expenses (those that may fluctuate, such as food, utilities, entertainment).

Housing – rent/mortgage	
Travel	
Food	
Utilities – gas, electric, water, council tax, phone, TV	
Entertainment	
Clothes and shoes	
Beauty treatments, e.g., hair, makeup, nails	
Debt payments	
Savings	

4. **Set spending limits.** Analyse your expenses and determine where you can cut back. Set realistic spending limits for each category based on your financial goals. Look for the leaks! How many times are you buying coffee, sandwiches or taking cabs? Be more mindful of discretionary spending and find areas where you can save.

5. **Allocate for savings and debt payments.** Prioritise saving for emergencies and paying off any high-interest debts. Allocate a portion of your income towards savings and debt repayment each month. The general rule of thumb is to save at least 10–20 per cent of your income.

6. **Use a budgeting tool.** Consider using a budgeting app or software to help you track your income and expenses automatically. These tools can also provide insights into your spending habits and help you stay on track.

7. **Review and adjust.** Monitor your budget regularly and review your progress. Make adjustments as necessary to ensure your budget aligns with your financial goals and current circumstances. If you consistently overspend in a particular category, consider reallocating funds from another area or finding ways to reduce expenses.

8. **Plan for the future.** Your budget should not only focus on your monthly expenses but also include long-term financial planning. Consider retirement savings, investments and other financial goals you may have.

9. **Be flexible and realistic.** Remember that your budget is not set in stone and can be adjusted over time. It's important to be flexible and adapt as your income or expenses change. Be realistic in your expectations and make gradual changes to your spending habits for long-term success.

By following these steps, you can create a comprehensive financial budget that helps you manage your money effectively and work towards your financial goals.

Building Your Credit Score

What is a credit score?

A credit score is a tool used by lenders to assess whether you qualify for a particular type of credit, be it a loan, mortgage, credit card, mobile phone or car finance. Every time you apply for credit, each lender uses your financial history and current credit obligations to predict your future behaviour. Their job is to decide if you will be able to repay the total credit amount you are asking for.

Why do you need a good credit score?

Credit scores are an essential part of your financial health. You need a good credit score to access loans, credit cards or other forms of credit on the lowest possible interest rates. Those with lower credit scores may be denied credit or could be offered unfavourable terms, usually involving a higher interest rate.

It is vital to understand your current credit score before you apply for any credit. This will help determine if you would meet a company's criteria. Many credit score companies can now offer pre-approved offers on loans, credit cards and finance based on your credit score to avoid complicated searches and possible refusals that would negatively impact your score.

What information do lenders use?

Lenders collate a variety of data around your lending history and lifestyle factors such as:

- Your current amount of debt
- The number of credit searches and applications you have made in the last 12 months
- Your current credit obligations (e.g., contract phones, loans, credit card balances, car loans)
- Whether you pay balances in full or miss any payments
- Debt-to-income ratio – how much do you owe versus your income, so you are not overstretching yourself
- Employment history
- Whether you own your home and how long you have lived there
- Public records (electoral roll and county court judgments).

Essentially, lenders are making an assessment on your ability to pay back the debt. They are more likely to lend to people who pay their bills on time, have a trackable employment and housing history and are registered on the electoral roll.

How do you check your credit score?

A credit score is a three-digit number calculated by applying a mathematical algorithm developed by Experian, TransUnion and Equifax, taken from the information in your credit reports.

These are updated every time any of the above criteria changes. The way you manage your monthly payments (this includes monthly household bills like utilities as well as any other credit agreements) is reflected in your rating.

You have the right to access your credit score without having to pay or subscribe to a service. Anybody can gain free access through the following websites: Clearscore, Experian, Credit Karma and Money Supermarket Credit Monitor.

However, if you need further details behind these scores you will need to pay. For example, you might want to know the specific issues negatively impacting your score. By paying for a premium account with a credit reference agency you will be able to see a comprehensive credit report.

How you can improve your credit score

If your score is lower than you would like, don't worry! You can do several things to improve it. Here are some top tips for helping you get a star credit rating:

1. Use other forms of credit. This may sound strange, but think about it. A credit agency must have some history to predict your future behaviour. If you don't have other loans or credit cards, they have little information to go on. So, use credit within sensible limits.

2. Make your monthly payments on time. Make it a priority to pay all your monthly bills and credit payments on time. Late and missed payments have a detrimental effect on your credit score. Create a monthly budget so you know exactly what you have to pay before calculating your disposable income for everything else. The more disciplined you are, the better your score will be.

3. Make sure your personal details are correct. Ensure your address is correct and that you are listed on the electoral roll. Errors in address or not appearing on the roll make a significant impact on your score. If you do spot any errors, inform the credit agency immediately so your record can be corrected.

4. Use credit but not too much. We advised above to use other forms of credit. What is equally important is that you do not use too much. Credit agencies review how much of your total available credit you use at any time. So, if you have a credit limit of £4,000 on your credit card and your current balance is £3,000, you are at 75 per cent utilisation.

If your credit cards are maxed out, you have additional loans and a high mortgage, your credit score will be lower than for someone who is using credit sensibly. To increase your credit score, reduce your credit utilisation to below 50 per cent. The best scores are generally applied to people using no more than 30 per cent.

5. Share your bank account with your credit agency. If you link your bank account with a credit agency, they will be able to get much clearer insights into your monthly transactions and levels of income. This helps lenders make more accurate decisions about how much you can afford to borrow at the best rates they can offer. You must provide your consent to your bank to set up this link.

6. Get a credit-building credit card. If you have had some financial difficulties in recent years and want to increase your credit score, a credit-building card can be an effective tool to help you along the way. You are more likely to be approved for these cards but must accept that you will pay much higher rates of interest than standard cards.

The key to using a credit-building card is to pay off your monthly balance in full every month. If you can do this, you can accelerate the rebuilding of your credit score without facing high interest payments.

Monitoring your credit score

Monitoring your credit rating will also help you keep control of your financial situation. A bad credit rating is likely to be the barrier between you and a mortgage, loans or even car finance. Doing so also allows you to identify any potentially fraudulent credit applications on your file. If you do find one, contact the credit agency immediately and report it. Monitoring your score allows you to be more conscious of what you are spending and the key areas you need to prioritise to help you improve your score.

If you spot any activity on your credit report that you do not recognise, report this immediately as you could have been exposed to identity fraud.

Why staying on top of your debts is essential

Credit cards make it easy for people to buy things when they can't necessarily afford them. Consumers often lose track of their total outlay and, before long, face spiralling debts. Unfortunately, these debts will always need to be repaid and often include high rates of interest. Paying the minimum amount means you barely touch the outstanding balance. It is best if you aim to pay your credit cards in full each month, strengthening your credit score at the same time.

- It is vital to keep track of how much you are borrowing. It gets harder, the more credit cards you have. Rather than treating them separately, you need to remember that the overall total is the actual debt you have.
- Make sure you read the terms and conditions of your credit card. If you have a credit card with 0% interest, ensure you know how long you have before the interest-free period is over.
- Other debts might include furniture on "Buy Now Pay Later" schemes, kitchens, bathrooms – the list of companies offering credit is endless. Think carefully before increasing your debts – ideally wait for the item and save for it.
- Always make sure you pay all your household bills and debt repayments on time. Defaulting will cause issues with your credit status.

- Never allow yourself to get into a situation that results in a county court judgment or seriously high arrears – they create a huge impact on your credit score for years to come.

Managing Debt Issues

If you have allowed your spending to get out of control and are now in debt, please read this section carefully and work towards moving yourself out of the situation.

The burden of financial problems can make you feel stressed and depressed. Debt can dramatically affect your mental health. Financial worries are the sixth most common cause of stress. Feelings of lack of control and impending disaster are significant contributors to depression and anxiety. The fears caused by debt problems make it significantly harder to focus on a solution.

So, what should you do if you are in this situation?

Here are some tips and advice to help.

Symptoms of debt issues

It's vital to recognise that anyone can undergo money issues during their lives. Children are rarely taught how to manage money at home or school, so it is unsurprising that so many experience major problems as they get older. It is vital to teach children good financial habits from a young age. We have discussed ways to do this in Chapter 4.

If you find yourself with any of the symptoms below, it is time to act:

- Are you only making minimum payments every month, but your balance keeps growing?
- Be honest with yourself: how much do you owe?
- Do you ignore the phone when the debt collectors call?

- Are you ignoring bills?
- Do you have little or no savings?
- Have you been applying for another credit card when the ones you have are maxed out?
- Does thinking about your repayments make you feel anxious or depressed?
- Have you been denied loans or credit cards?
- Are you making excuses for your financial situation?
- Have you withdrawn from your friends and family?
- Do you find it hard to concentrate at work?
- Is your sleep being disrupted due to money worries?

Improving your mental health

With debt problems hanging over you, the chances are this will be affecting your mental health. Poor mental health affects one in four adults in the UK and is commonly associated with financial problems. Research shows that 50 per cent of adults in the UK who experience money difficulties also suffer from poor mental health.

Please remember you are not alone. There are organisations that can help you create a plan to reduce your debt and support your well-being while you work to do this. The first step to improve the situation is to get help.

If you have a friend or family member who stays objective and listens to you, start by talking to them. If you are too embarrassed to discuss your problems with them, there are organisations that will support you. The organisations below provide lots of advice and options for taking steps to improve your situation.[4]

For mental health support:

Mind – www.mind.org.uk
Mental Health Foundation – www.mentalhealth.org.uk

---

4. These are UK organisations; similar organisations are available in other countries.

For free debt advice:

Citizens Advice Bureau – www.citizensadvice.org.uk
National Debtline – www.nationaldebtline.org
Step Change – www.stepchange.org

The help is there. Reach out and take a step towards getting your finances under control, which in turn will help your mental health. Do not be tempted by payday loans or consolidation loans.

This will inevitably make matters worse and leave you in even more debt.

Whilst debt issues can seem overwhelming, there is always light at the end of the tunnel. You just need the right help.

Resolving your debt issues

The first step is calculating how much you owe in total, then you will be able to devise an effective strategy to reduce your debt.

The first step – what do you owe?
- Calculate your current outstanding debt (overdrafts, loans and credit cards).
- Create a monthly bill payment calendar.
- Make at least the minimum payment.
- Prioritise which debts to pay off first; target the ones with the highest interest rate.

Next step – create more income to clear your debts
- Use a monthly budget to plan your expenses.
- Shop in budget supermarkets and pound-stores rather than paying more for premium brands. Most sell similar quality products for significantly less money.
- Allocate a period when you will only buy essential items. Stop buying clothes, gadgets and anything else you don't actually need.

- Look at what you have in your wardrobe or around your house that you could sell to raise additional cash.
- Stop spending money on coffees and lunches. Take a packed lunch instead. Reduce spending on entertainment.

Use the money you are saving to repay debt each month.
For example, a takeaway coffee and sandwich for lunch each day costs around £8.00. Over a year (taking out four weeks' holiday), that would cost you £1,920. And that's without the cake and crisps!

Remember, getting out of debt is never insurmountable. It may be challenging, and it may take time, but you can get there with the right plan and support. Getting the right advice and an expert to be subjective about your situation is the most important thing you can do to help plan a clear path for the future.

Saving and Investing

Starting to save money is an important step towards financial stability and achieving your long-term goals.

Here are some steps to help you get started with saving:

1. Set clear goals. Determine why you want to save money. It could be for an emergency fund, buying a house, starting a business or retirement. Having specific goals will help you stay motivated and focused.

2. Create a budget. Track your income and expenses to understand your financial situation. Identify areas where you can reduce expenses and allocate a portion of your income towards savings. Make sure to prioritise saving as a regular expense in your budget.

3. Automate savings. Set up an automatic transfer from your current account to a separate savings account each month. This way, you won't have to rely on willpower alone to save money – it will happen automatically.

4. Increase income. Explore opportunities to increase your income, such as taking on a side job or freelancing, negotiating a raise at work, or developing additional skills to enhance your earning potential.

5. Track your progress. Regularly review your savings progress to stay motivated and make adjustments if needed. Celebrate milestones along the way to maintain your enthusiasm.

6. Educate yourself. Learn about personal finance, investing and saving strategies. There are numerous resources available, including books, articles, podcasts and online courses that can help you develop better financial habits and make informed decisions (refer to the resources section at the back of this book).

> **Remember, saving money is a habit that requires consistency and discipline.**

Start small and gradually increase your savings over time. The key is to get started and stay committed to your savings goals.

Mortgages

When buying your first home there is a lot to consider. The first thing is to work out how much money you will need to buy a property and if you can afford the mortgage payments. Typically, most lenders require a deposit of 5–10 per cent of the purchase price.

You will also need to factor in legal costs, survey, mortgage valuation fees and stamp duty[5] where relevant. How much you can borrow will depend on your income; different lenders having varying policies.

---

5. Stamp Duty Land Tax (SDLT) is payable in the UK on increasing portions of the property price when you buy residential property, for example a house or flat.

Use an online mortgage calculator to determine how much you can borrow, be realistic and don't overstretch yourself.

A good credit score is crucial for mortgage approval. Check your credit report, correct any errors and work on improving your score; you can find out more in the section above. Bad credit of any kind can prevent you from getting a mortgage approved, so ensure you make payments on your commitments each month. Even with previous credit issues you may still be able to get a mortgage, but the range of products will be limited, and rates might be higher.

When applying for a mortgage, a broker who is whole-of-market can often help you get the best deals. Ask family or friends for a referral or find someone online (but check their reviews first).

You can get a mortgage agreed in principle, called an AIP, before you start viewing properties, a clear benefit when you come to making an offer.

To apply for a mortgage the lender will require:

- Proof of name and address including a recent utility bill
- Bank statement from within the past three months
- Photo ID (passport or driving licence)
- Some may request your last three payslips.

Saving for your deposit

Currently you could investigate opening a Lifetime ISA (LISA) if you are aged between 18 and 39. You can use it to save up to £4,000 a year, towards either a first home costing up to £450,000 or for retirement. You have the bonus that the state will add a 25 per cent bonus on top of what you save, meaning an additional £1,000 of free cash annually. Plus, you earn interest on whatever you save, and as it's an ISA, that interest is tax free.

The UK government offers various help-to-buy schemes aimed at assisting first-time buyers and home movers. Research these schemes to see if you qualify.

I haven't gone into any more details about mortgages in this book because it's such a vast subject. My advice, as always, is to talk to a reputable mortgage broker and seek their help.

Investing

Investing your money into long-term investments will mean your money will be tied up for longer periods to get a better return.

So only do this once you have an emergency fund set up and have cleared any debt.

Investing should only be considered once you have taken care of your basic financial needs.

The first step is to clarify your investment goals
Are you investing for retirement, a down payment on a house, or another specific purpose?

Knowing your goals will help determine the appropriate investment timeline and risk tolerance.

What is your investment time horizon?
Consider your investment time horizon – the length of time you expect to invest before needing the money. Generally, longer time horizons allow for a higher tolerance for market fluctuations and potentially higher returns. If you have a shorter time horizon, you may need to opt for more conservative investment options.

Assess your risk tolerance
This is important, as it explores your ability to withstand market fluctuations and potential investment losses. Investments come with varying levels of risk, and it's important to invest in a way that aligns with your comfort level.

Knowledge and research

Educate yourself about investing and different investment options. Understand the basics of asset classes, diversification and risk management. Consult with a financial advisor to help you make informed investment decisions.

It's worth noting that investing is a long-term commitment, and it's generally recommended to start as early as possible. By starting early, you can take advantage of the power of compounding and potentially benefit from the growth of your investments over time. However, it's essential to strike a balance between investing and meeting your immediate financial needs.

Pensions Retirement Planning

Sadly, many women are unprepared for retirement. The Pension Gap is a major issue for many women, who have a fraction of what their male counterparts have in their pension pot. This can be because they have taken time out to raise a family, had lower paid jobs or have been divorced. Therefore, saving money into a pension is vital if you want to live a comfortable life in retirement.

Many women do not place a strong emphasis on having their own private pension. Over the years I have lost count of the number of times women have said to me they don't need to worry about a pension. Too often I hear that their husband or partner has a good pension and that will be enough. However, if you get divorced, you become a widow or your spouse becomes ill and no longer works, this will leave you with potentially serious financial issues in retirement.

The state pension will help you survive, but that is all it is designed to do. The age when you can claim a pension keeps shifting and it's quite possible that the state pension might disappear at some point in the future.

A pension will secure your financial future, helping you maintain your standard of living once you retire without having to sell your home or dip into other savings.

It is important to set one up if you are running your own business – there are tax benefits.

All employers must offer you a pension scheme and I would advise making additional contributions to this if you can.

I am regularly taken aback when people tell me they decided not to take out a pension or opted out of one. Their general view is that "life is for living"; retirement seems so far in the future. Sadly, many people build very small pension funds, creating poor outcomes for them in retirement.

It's worth noting that your private pension pot does not include the state pension paid by the government. Therefore, the more money you save now, the more money you will have to spend in the future.

If, like most people, you have worked for more than one employer during your career, you will almost certainly have multiple funds. All of these funds will be contributing to your retirement income, so we will talk about how to review your total pension pot below.

People often ask me if it is worth having a pension. My response is always the same. In my 30 years as a financial advisor, not one of my retired clients has ever said to me, "I'm really disappointed that I've got a pension."

One of my clients illustrates that getting advice and acting on it makes a huge difference.

> Lindsay said: "I met Diane when she spoke at a seminar about pensions for women about 20 years ago. This made me think about my pension arrangements, and I learnt a lot. At the time pensions were a bit of a mystery to me. After getting proper advice from Diane, she urged me to go with my company pension scheme. I hadn't taken this opportunity as I was concerned there might be a catch (which there wasn't!). That fund is now my main pension pot. I would have continued to bury my head in the sand if I had not attended that event.
>
> She also suggested a range of investment options to me based on my attitude to risk which is very risk averse! The money I saved at the time and promptly forgot about is now worth over six times its original value. I would simply never have made that investment without Diane's knowledge and advice, so thank you very much."

Why invest in a pension?

You are never too young to start investing in a pension. They are not something to put off until you have kids, a mortgage and plenty of other bills. The earlier you start, the more you will save for a prosperous future. You could start a pension for your child now!

In my experience, a lot of people give little thought to their later years.

Ask yourself:

- When will you be mortgage-free?
- How much money do you think you will need each month to pay your bills?
- Do you have dreams to travel, buy a holiday home or take up an expensive hobby?
- How much money will you need every month to live the life you want?

And remember, we are living longer than ever before.

Once you stop working for an employer or running your own business, you still need an income unless you have saved a very large sum of money. That is why pensions are so important. Your monthly contributions grow by being invested in funds designed to deliver returns that match your attitude to risk. You also enjoy the added benefit of tax relief on your contributions. This means some of the money you would have given the treasury is invested in your pension instead. Your pension provider or financial advisor will update you at least annually on how your fund is performing and what your retirement income is likely to be.

How do you start a pension?

Many employers now offer to automatically enrol employees into workplace pension schemes. If you get offered automatic enrolment, this means a percentage of your salary gets deducted and put into a pension pot for you. Even better, your employer also contributes a percentage! Whilst it may look like you are losing out on some of your pay each month, this is an investment that will help secure your future.

Some employers will offer you a Group Personal Pension scheme. This scheme will be managed by a pension provider chosen by your employer, offering lower costs because of the number of people they cover. However, the pension will be a direct arrangement between you and the pension provider. Typically, your employer will normally pay a monthly contribution into your pension. Indeed, some people consider how much an employer contributes to their pension as a key factor in deciding whether to work for a company. There are various schemes with different benefits. It's worth taking the time to understand what scheme you are part of and the benefits it delivers.

If you are knowledgeable about investments, or use a financial advisor, you may choose to invest into a self-invested personal pension (SIPP). It is very similar to the standard personal pension but gives you extra flexibility and control over where your pension fund is invested.

Why you need to review your pension

Once you have been paying into your pension for some time, it is important to review how it is performing on a regular basis. That way you can ensure you are on track for your retirement plans.

It is easy to set up your pension scheme and then forget about it. The fact is, you may change your appetite for risk as you get older, have more or less money to invest, or your funds may be underperforming. That is why it is essential that you review your pension pot at least annually.

This is even more important if you have several pension funds. Make note of all your pension schemes so you can calculate your total pot. Furthermore, you have the opportunity to review integrating your pensions into one fund for convenience, ease of tracking and increased performance. It is important to note that you should check the terms and conditions of the various schemes to ensure you do not lose out on any benefits from different providers.

Questions to ask when reviewing your pension

- Have your retirement goals changed? If so, do you need to increase your contributions, increase your retirement age or move to a higher performing fund?
- Are you prepared to take more risk to enjoy potentially higher returns? If so, you may wish to move your investments.
- Do you want to reduce your risk as you get closer to retirement?
- Have you changed employers or become self-employed? If so, get the right advice about starting your own personal pension scheme or whether to move your existing pensions into your new employer's fund.

Get advice on your pension

It is well worth getting a financial advisor to help you review your pensions and make the right investment decisions.

Advisors from the pension companies cannot give you advice themselves; they can only answer your factual questions.

If you are interested in finding out more about your pension pot, the MoneyHelper pension calculator[6] is a good place to review your current situation. You can also check at what age you will be able to receive your state pension via the UK government website.

Hopefully, you can now see that investing in a pension is essential to leading a happy and prosperous retirement. It may seem like years away. But time passes very quickly. So please – if you don't have a pension, start one now. And if you do, have you reviewed it lately?

Where are you currently? You can check your UK state pension forecast here: https://www.gov.uk/check-state-pension

Lost pensions

If you have pensions you have lost the details for you can check the Pension Tracing Service which is a free government service. It searches a database of more than 200,000 workplace and personal pension schemes to try to find the contact details you need.

You can phone the Pension Tracing Service on 0800 731 0193 or use the following link to search their online directory for contact details: www.gov.uk/find-pension-contact-details

---

6. https://www.moneyhelper.org.uk/en/pensions-and-retirement/pensions-basics/pension-calculator

Pensions are not just for retirement

Pensions, whilst the main source of income for retirement, can be accessed currently at age 55 (in April 2028 this will increase to 57).

You can access 25 per cent of your fund tax free; any other income you take from your pension fund is taxable. Whilst the greatest benefit to maximising your pension fund is to leave your pension until you are retiring, there might be reasons you need to access the money earlier.

To highlight how important a pension can be, not just in retirement but to support you later in life, here is a story from Catherine about her pension experience.

STARTING A PENSION EARLY REAPS REWARDS

Catherine's story

Catherine is a successful employment lawyer who has had an interest in finance since her teenage years. This interest has allowed her to accumulate a pension that is supporting her in her 50s as well as providing for her retirement years. She explains her attitude to building a pension fund, and how she directly controls the investments in her scheme.

Catherine has been a lawyer throughout her working life. She started work as a self-employed barrister before becoming an in-house lawyer at 25. Her career developed, and she became a successful employment lawyer for over 30 years.

Catherine embraced pension savings from the start of her career. She is passionate about taking control of her fund, having managed her investments in conjunction with her financial advisors. Her pension pot has allowed her to buy a house whilst maintaining a retirement fund. Her story shows there are many options regarding pensions, but ultimately that everyone has a choice.

Catherine's background

Catherine came from a home where her mother worked as a teacher, and her electrical engineer father was fascinated with investing in shares. It was a solid grounding for a young girl who went on to study economics at A Level. She was unusual in her taste in TV programmes, watching the likes of *The Money Programme* and *Moneybox* with great interest.

Her dad retired at 54, having benefited from a gold-plated public-sector pension scheme, but sadly died aged just 67. Luckily Catherine's mother had her teacher's pensions to fall back on, coupled with her widow's pension from her husband's scheme, providing a healthy monthly income in addition to her state pension entitlement. But her dad utilised his tax-free lump sum to invest in shares etc. and therefore also left an investment portfolio that her mother had to manage. As Catherine says: "My mum hated it. She found it incredibly difficult." Yet Catherine has clearly inherited her father's interest in finance. She took the same hands-on approach with her pension.

Starting a pension early

Catherine entered a final salary scheme with defined benefits when she started working. These pensions could pay out a higher amount than a standard pension. Moving to a law firm gave her access to a defined contribution scheme. But within three years, she became an equity partner. Now self-employed, she could no longer participate in the company scheme. It became her responsibility to arrange her own pension.

Knowing this was likely given her career path, Catherine was prepared to invest. She found a financial advisor she trusted, believing the proper guidance was imperative to achieving the best results. But as she says: "You have to be vaguely interested in where your money's going. No one looks at it like you do." Since starting her pension, Catherine has taken complete control of her fund. Whilst she has enlisted the help of financial advisors, she keeps a close check on progress and makes changes where necessary.

Teaching her child about pensions

In her late 30s, Catherine gave birth to her son, Thomas. In the process, she developed gestational diabetes, a condition she still suffers from. And one that would have an impact in other ways.

As a single parent, Catherine took responsibility for helping her son understand financial matters. She was also determined he grew up financially independent. "I set up Thomas with a small pension when he was born. That was topped up with a Child Trust Fund. He now has a pot of over £80,000." Catherine's mother supplemented the fund, having saved regularly for him.

Now in a solid financial position, Thomas has just completed his first year at university, funded by Catherine and his father. He has had a part-time job for the last few years, and when he turned 18, Catherine introduced him to her financial advisor. Thus, he took control of his fund: "I hope he doesn't go and buy a fast car, although I can't stop him. But so far, he's been sensible."

Using your pension before retirement

After over 25 years working as an employment lawyer, Catherine has gone into partnership with her own business, McBrownie Ltd. She provides outsourced employment services and consultancy to SMEs. But starting her own business had a further impact on her life as she was unable to secure a mortgage due to her recent self-employed status.

However, what she was able to do was access some of her pension fund, tax free. Combined with her savings, she was able to purchase the forever house. This illustrates how pension funds can be used for life's milestone moments, as well as being used for retirement income. Whilst it reduced her fund, she maintains having no mortgage at this stage of her life is beneficial.

"I have a different view to many people about pensions. As a diabetic, I have no idea how long I have. But I look at my dad's life and think I should make the most of my time now."

Catherine demonstrates that personal finance must be tailored to individual needs. "My take on pensions is I have been saving for my life today. Many believe retirement is a long way off, so the pension shouldn't be touched. My experience is that if you save early and build a decent pot, you will have sufficient funds to extract money in your late 50s while still keeping a reasonable retirement fund."

Catherine has since used further sums to buy a car and a new kitchen. She has no intention of spending all her money. However, as we have seen, she is determined to use the pot she has accumulated today as well as tomorrow.

Catherine's current financial status

Now 57, Catherine has no mortgage and is happily married for the third time, living in Scotland. She has a will, but there are gaps in her portfolio: "I can't get critical illness or income protection because of my diabetes." However, with a sizeable pension fund and the equity in her house, there is enough to fall back on should she need it. A continuing power of attorney, as it's called in Scotland, also needs to be implemented.

Contributions to her pension ceased when she became self-employed. She has some flexibility with future contributions especially since the April 2023 budget limits were increased. Nobody needs to tell her how important saving into a pension is. Further contributions may be added.

Working towards retirement

Currently, Catherine aims to retire at 67. However, she keeps an open mind: "At the moment, my health is fine. But that's not guaranteed." She outlines other considerations: "My mum is in her 80s, and I recognise I may need to spend more time with her. My husband is six years older than me. He, too, may develop health problems. Any of those issues could influence when I give up work."

Today, Catherine is working around two days a week. She has the flexibility to spend time with her family, including her stepdaughter, who lives in Cornwall.

But retaining an income means she can avoid drawing down on her pension. It also allows her to offer her HR expertise to a grateful SME market.

Catherine's advice to young women

As you will have gleaned from this story, Catherine is passionate about pension saving. She advises people to start saving from a young age and, importantly, to get good advice. "I've had three financial advisors over the years. The first two both retired. I now have an advisor who is 20 years younger than me!"

She is clear: **find an advisor who meets your needs**. In her case, she identified qualified and registered advisors who could support her investment strategies.

Catherine is adamant that even if you are in your 50s, there is always time to start saving. It's better to do something than nothing at all. But she also carefully considers younger people: "Personal finance should be taught at school, especially pension saving. We need better advice for people of all ages so they understand their options."

Catherine is not typical of many savers. She has relished being in control of her investments from the very start. Taking large sums from her retirement fund may not be suitable for everyone. But she shows that people face different circumstances. Accessing a large pot of money she has spent years growing has made a significant impact in recent years. Added to the state pension, Catherine is still on track to have a retirement income of £3,000 a month. More than enough, considering she has no mortgage and grown children who are financially independent.

POINTS FOR PROSPERITY

Create your budget – use our guide in this chapter.

_____

_____

_____

_____

What are your top 3 financial goals?

1. _____

2. _____

3. _____

What is your credit score? What one thing can you do to improve it?

_____

_____

_____

_____

How much debt do you have in total?

_____

_____

_____

_____

If you don't have one, start a pension. How much can you save a month?

_____

_____

_____

_____

If you haven't already, start saving. How much can you save each month?

_____

_____

_____

_____

CHAPTER THREE

Protecting Your Prosperity

"Protect what you have built from life's unexpected events." - Diane Watson

As you go through life, buy a home and create savings, it's important to consider what would happen if you couldn't work due to illness or injury.

Being unable to work, even for a few months, can have a significant impact on your ability to pay your bills. If your illness results in long-term sickness or permanent disability, the results for your finances can be catastrophic.

It's important to understand and evaluate what protection policies are available to cover your income and decide what best suits your needs. This will depend on your circumstances and whether you are employed or work for yourself.

I have shared in this chapter some information on critical illness cover, income protection and life insurance. Plus, some stories of people who needed to utilise their policies.

There are ways of reducing premiums, for example a joint policy with your partner. However, bear in mind that once there is a claim, your policy is terminated. This will mean your partner will need to find new cover, potentially facing increased premiums.

You might also consider saving by combining life and critical illness cover. But again, once there is a claim, the policy is finished. In these situations, it can leave you without life cover and, after dealing with a critical illness such as cancer, expensive life insurance premiums.

My advice is some cover is better than no cover at all. Make sure you fully understand what policy you are implementing, its implications and the risks involved.

Critical Illness Cover

Critical illness cover is an insurance policy that provides financial protection to individuals and their families in the event of a serious illness. The policy pays out a lump sum if the policyholder is diagnosed with a specific critical illness, as defined in the policy terms.

The importance of critical illness cover cannot be overstated, as a serious illness can have devastating consequences, not just for the individual but also for their family. The financial impact of a critical illness can be significant, as it can result in loss of income, increased medical expenses and other related costs.

Having a critical illness cover can provide a sense of security and peace of mind, as it can help to alleviate some of the financial burden associated with a critical illness. It can help individuals to focus on their recovery without worrying about the financial implications.

Moreover, the likelihood of being diagnosed with a critical illness is higher than one might expect. According to research, one in two people will develop cancer in their lifetime, and one in three people will develop cardiovascular disease.

Critical illness cover will give you peace of mind and can help you prepare for the unexpected and protect your financial future.

There are organisations that can help support you if you do contract cancer or other life-limiting illnesses. One such organisation is Maggie's Cancer Centres, a charity I hold in very high regard, having seen first-hand the support they have given to friends.

Dame Laura Lee, its Chief Executive, said: "You may expect that a cancer diagnosis will impact finances because you may need to give up work or take on less hours. But it can also bring additional, unexpected costs for things like travel to appointments, child and pet care, household chores and even a change in diet or skincare. These are the costs that add up over time and can eat into savings. Unfortunately, financial support doesn't always cover everything, meaning people are left struggling and out of pocket."

You will find their details in the back of this book alongside other organisations that can help.

Healthy people do get sick!

Approximately one in three people will be diagnosed with a serious illness that will affect their ability to work. So many people think, because they lead a healthy lifestyle, they won't become ill. Unfortunately, I work with women who prove this is a fallacy.

DON'T CANCEL YOUR CRITICAL ILLNESS COVER

Amy's story

Amy nearly cancelled her critical illness cover when she was made redundant. Thankfully she didn't. Weeks later she was diagnosed with breast cancer, and critical illness cover proved invaluable.

If there is a story that best illustrates why everyone should have critical illness cover, it is Amy's. In the summer of 2022, Amy found a lump in her breast. It was diagnosed as cancerous and within weeks she had a lumpectomy. Sadly, there are other stories like this in the book. What sets Amy apart is the fact that she was out of work at the time. She was considering ceasing her critical illness policy but chose not to. A crucial, and correct, decision, as it turned out.

Amy is married with two children in primary school. After a career working in both the public and private sector, she was made redundant in 2014. She decided to become a self-employed business change consultant. Her husband was also self-employed, so having lost her corporate benefits package, the couple had to think hard about their financial situation.

As self-employed people facing unpredictability and no safety net, both took out critical illness and life insurance policies. Amy is clear: critical illness cover is not cheap; her policy was costing £77 a month and there were times when she contemplated cancelling it. She went back to employment for a time then decided to leave and it was whilst deciding on what to do next she received a shocking diagnosis.

The benefit of retaining critical illness cover

One day Amy found a lump in her breast. Within weeks she had a lumpectomy, an early diagnosis meaning the growth was still small. From November 2022, she faced hormone therapy that will be administered for between five and ten years. In December she had five days of radiotherapy "that completely floored me."

All of this was made more bearable as Amy could call on her critical illness policy. She was thankful she had retained the cover as it proved vital in her battle to recover from cancer.

"I called Legal and General the day after I received the diagnosis. There was a wait for the payout as the lump and surrounding tissues had to be assessed. The level of payment ranged from 25 to 100 per cent, depending on the severity. My cancer had spread so I received 100 per cent."

Alleviating financial stress

The fight against cancer has been mentally and physically tough for Amy. But the financial stress she felt following her diagnosis was alleviated following her payout. "I was on employment support allowance for the first few months – £117 a week. That didn't cover our food bill, let alone everything else."

Amy was planning to go back to work in March 2023, but that fell through. Under the circumstances she is relieved: "It was lucky, because I really wasn't well enough."

The lump sum replaced her income and allowed her to pay off 10 per cent of her mortgage. It also meant she could save a substantial amount, providing some peace of mind, given her physical health and the state of the employment market.

Amy's advice to young women

Amy is a woman who, like everyone else, never believed cancer would happen to her. Her maternal grandmother had been a sufferer in her 60s, but that was the only instance in her family. She had often questioned whether critical illness was a waste of money.

Now she is emphatic: **"Breast cancer is affecting women younger and younger. Don't take the risk. Get covered."** She admits, "I was the principal earner in our family with two young kids. We also owned rental properties. It's why I decided to keep critical illness in place. We set up a joint policy that ensured all the mortgages would be paid off. It was so worth it."

She makes this point: "Without critical illness, we would have ploughed through our savings. Now we have a savings pot that can support us for some time to come – vital when recovering from cancer."

Income Protection

This is a type of insurance that provides financial protection in the event that you are unable to work, due to an illness or disability. It aims to replace a portion of the insured person's income to help them maintain their standard of living and cover essential expenses during their period of incapacity.

Income protection policies typically cover a wide range of illnesses, disabilities and injuries that prevent a person from working. They may include both physical and mental health conditions, as long as they meet the policy's specific criteria.

The policyholder can choose the level of benefit they want to receive, usually expressed as a percentage of their pre-disability income. It's important to note that policies have a maximum limit on the percentage of income that can be replaced to prevent over-insurance.

Income protection policies have a waiting period, also known as a deferred period, which is the period of time the policyholder must be unable to work before they become eligible to receive benefits. The waiting period can range from a few weeks to several months, and a longer waiting period often results in lower premium costs. Policies can provide benefits for a specific duration, such as two years, five years or until retirement age. The longer the benefit payment period, the higher the premium is likely to be.

The cost of an income protection policy is determined by various factors, including the individual's age, health, occupation, chosen benefit amount, waiting period and benefit payment duration. Premiums can be paid monthly or annually.

Income protection benefits are usually tax free, which means the payments received under the policy are not subject to income tax.

It's important to carefully review the terms and conditions of different income protection policies to ensure they meet your specific needs and circumstances. Consulting a qualified financial advisor or insurance specialist can help you navigate the options available and make an informed decision.

THE IMPORTANCE OF CRITICAL ILLNESS AND INCOME PROTECTION

Eleanor's story

I wanted to highlight women in this book who best illustrate why I advocate the financial strategies I do. Eleanor is a perfect case in point. She and her husband used the services of a financial advisor before they were even married in their 20s. They followed all the advice I gave. But life is unpredictable, and sadly, Eleanor contracted a chronic medical condition that has put constant challenges in her way. But having the proper financial protection has allowed her to manage the condition and change her life.

Eleanor was always a planner. As a young woman, she created vision boards to design her future and set goals, personal and financial. When she married, her husband wanted similar things: a nice house, a couple of children, successful careers and financial security.

Her story illustrates how unpredictable life can be. And how careful financial planning provides choices that can help when being diagnosed with a chronic medical condition.

Financial planning started early

Eleanor has always been sensible with money. Her parents encouraged her to be a saver from a young age. In her first post-graduate job, she recalls a session for new staff about pensions: "Everyone there seemed disinterested, but I was fascinated!" Eleanor recognised she had a different mindset towards money from that of her friends and associates. She credits this to her mother, an inveterate saver who passed this habit on.

When Eleanor and her husband were in their early 20s, they met with a financial advisor for the first time. "We weren't earning huge amounts, but we already had our first house, and both had company cars. We considered we were doing well", remembered Eleanor. Her financial advisor helped them set up life cover, something they extended several years later when they had children. Indeed, having children prompted her to take out numerous forms of financial protection policies.

Eleanor and her husband, Glyn, were ambitious and successful in their careers. Eleanor loved her job in sales for a medical equipment company. The role took her all over Europe, earning a good salary, bonuses and a strong portfolio of employee benefits. Glyn quickly progressed to become director of a food company working in FMCG (fast-moving consumer goods). Like Eleanor, he was in a fast-paced, stressful job that delivered high rewards. At that time, Eleanor knew life was good: "Our only financial stress was to ring our financial advisor and get her to put an extra £20,000 in our pensions before the end of the tax year to minimise our tax bills."

By 2008, Eleanor and Glyn were well on their way to achieving their life goals. They had moved into a large barn conversion which required updating to create their perfect home and they had two young children. The couple had savings, they followed careers they loved and life was good.

But in 2008, things took a dark turn. Eleanor could not open her mouth to speak one morning after a friend's wedding. Whilst friends thought this amusing, Eleanor was understandably concerned. A few days later, she started to experience terrible pain in her hands. "I was working with medical specialists at that time," recounts Eleanor. "I'd stand observing foot surgery and noticed acute pain coming from my feet." The orthopaedic surgeon advised her to get checked out. Weeks later, she was in Bordeaux working with a knee surgeon and could barely walk. "He immediately told me to get tested by a rheumatologist," says Eleanor. Following those tests, she was diagnosed with rheumatoid arthritis, a chronic condition that causes extreme joint pain and swelling.

Dealing with a chronic illness

She found the language around rheumatoid arthritis was almost wholly negative: "life-changing" and "life-limiting". When she read the statistics, Eleanor was further alarmed – one in five people diagnosed with the condition would not be working within two years.

Eleanor recalls, "I was only 34, and I felt like my life was drifting away from me."

Stress was a constant during that period, a potential trigger for her illness. She had two young children, a new house needing much work, her mother had contracted a brain condition, and her dad had recently died of a brain tumour.

One benefit was that a recent promotion had given her a company income protection policy and private medical insurance. At least she had something to fall back on.

However, coming to terms with rheumatoid arthritis was extremely challenging. The effect on Eleanor's mental health was as profound as its physical impact. "Work was my identity, and I felt it was being taken away from me."

After battling intense pain and fatigue, Eleanor had to stop working. During the time off, Eleanor also noticed that she had developed a tremor while standing still. Not only was this going to be challenging if returning to work, but it also hampered her ability to socialise or even go to the supermarket, where queues at the tills were a "nightmare".

Income protection creates choices

Having been off work for a year, Eleanor wanted to return to work as her joint pain was more under control. She attended back-to-work meetings where she was told she would have to go through a phased return. This made her international sales job impossible. Furthermore, it became increasingly obvious that standing wasn't going to be possible due to the tremor.

The company explained that the only way to deal with the issue was for her to change roles; it was suggested that perhaps compliance would suit her. "I didn't want to do that. I loved my role. And it gave me major rewards – a high salary, big bonuses, a company car and other benefits. And I was good at sales; it was what I loved to do," said Eleanor.

At this point, Eleanor consulted her ex-boss, now a close friend. "She told me to look into my benefits package. It was time to review my options if I couldn't continue in my current role. She was super supportive."

Eleanor remembers feeling a sense of being labelled when she had to leave her company for good. Whilst this was not good for her mental well-being, the blow was cushioned by a lump sum.

This allowed her to pay off the mortgage, leaving funds for investment. She used that money to build a small buy-to-let portfolio which created a replacement for part of her income. As Eleanor emphasised: "This wasn't just a salary; it's part of my pension too."

A new phase

Having spent some time at home with the children and getting heavily involved with the school PTA, Eleanor was itching to throw herself into a new venture.

She was passionate about interior design, so after completing an upholstery course, Eleanor purchased a curtains and blinds business. While she was doing something she loved, it was a struggle. "I'd consult with a client on a design, and then a huge roll of fabric would turn up. I couldn't lift it." The only way to get the job done was to enlist the help of her mum and husband. "They said to me, 'We don't all want to make curtains and blinds, Eleanor!'." Consequently, she had to consider her options.

Around this time, Glyn was also considering his future. Whilst he had achieved much in his career, he was heavily stressed in his role and ready for a change. When the two discussed things, they decided that running a business together was the perfect solution. It helped to know they had the buffer of their rental income. Glyn joined her curtains and blinds business, which they have gradually evolved into a leading interior design company.

Eleanor has recruited a team to deal with the additional responsibilities of running the business. She recognises her physical limitations, but she retains her portfolio of clients who have grown used to her care and expertise.

Making the most of life

Eleanor has become more accepting of her situation, and doesn't let it stop her from doing what she wants. "I wanted to take my daughter to Paris but wasn't sure I could manage. My friend's husband said a woman can't take a car on a ferry." That was all the motivation Eleanor needed to book the trip. Her only concern was how she'd manage walking when she got there.

By now, she had a disabled badge, another sign of her growing acceptance that she needed help. Eleanor hired a disability scooter, a particular advantage when she took her daughter to a theme park. "They gave me a band that avoided all the queues for the rides. I was embarrassed, but my daughter thought it was brilliant. She said, 'You're always whining about being in pain. I deserve this for putting up with you!'"

What advice would Eleanor give young women about building financial security?

People say to Eleanor she was lucky. Her view is quite different. "I had the right protection in place. I made a conscious decision that meant I could make a choice when things went wrong."

She encourages every woman to look at their goals and ensure they are saving to achieve them and, vitally, to put enough protection in place to cover all eventualities.

Eleanor could never have foreseen an illness changing her life at 33. Her protection provided the foundations to live a different but equally fulfilling life without compromising on her aspirations.

Eleanor concludes: "We know that by the time I'm 60, we'll be financially independent. We will also have the option to sell the business or put in someone to run it and take the share dividends. We're only in this position because we made considered decisions in our 20s."

There is a lesson here for anyone wanting to create their financial security.

Life Insurance

Life insurance is a financial tool designed to provide financial protection and support for your loved ones in the event of your death. The younger you start a policy, the cheaper it will be. Consider what you need the life insurance for. That will help you decide on the level of cover you require.

Here are some common reasons why people take out life insurance cover:

1. Replacing lost income. If you have dependants who rely on your income to cover daily living expenses, such as your spouse, children or ageing parents, life insurance can help replace your lost income and ensure they are financially supported after your passing.

2. Covering outstanding debts. The money can be used to pay off any outstanding debts you may have, such as a mortgage, personal loans or credit card debt. This prevents your loved ones from inheriting these financial obligations and potentially struggling to make payments.

3. Funeral and final expenses. Funerals and related expenses can be costly. Life insurance can provide funds to cover these immediate expenses, relieving your family of the financial burden during an already difficult time.

4. Education and future planning. If you have children, life insurance can be used to fund their education and ensure they have the means to pursue their goals and aspirations, even if you are no longer there to provide for them.

5. Estate planning and inheritance. Life insurance can be utilised as a tool for estate planning. It can help create liquidity to pay estate taxes, leaving more of your assets intact for your heirs.

6. Business continuation. Life insurance is often used by business owners to ensure the continuity of their business in the event of their death. It can provide funds to cover business expenses, pay off loans or facilitate the transfer of ownership to a successor.

7. Peace of mind. Life insurance offers peace of mind, knowing that your loved ones will be financially protected and provided for in case of your unexpected demise. It can provide a sense of security, knowing that your family will be able to maintain their lifestyle and meet their financial obligations.

Consulting with a financial advisor or insurance professional can help you make informed decisions about life insurance.

UNDERSTANDING FINANCIAL PROTECTION POLICIES

Hannah's story

Throughout this book, I advocate the need to have the proper financial protection in place. Hannah's story shows that you can have financial protection without properly understanding the implications if you make a claim. Not surprisingly, I urge you to take out critical illness and life cover, but make sure you fully understand your policy.

In January 2019, Hannah was experiencing blurry vision in her left eye. Normally she would have left it a while. But needing to drive her children safely from one place to another motivated her to book an eye test. Hannah's optician proved thorough. She spotted something she was not happy with and referred her patient to St James's University Hospital in Leeds. Their checks led to another referral to Sheffield Eye Hospital. Hannah was diagnosed with an ocular melanoma, a rare cancer. Within three weeks, aged just 38, her eye was removed.

In 2022, Hannah was diagnosed with capillary thyroid cancer. She has had half her thyroid removed and is being monitored for future cancer cell growth. Should the worst happen, she will lose her whole thyroid and have radiation therapy.

These two events have had an enormous impact on her life. As a young woman, she did not expect to be facing such life-changing illnesses. What is also significant is the effect on Hannah's financial protection policies. This story explains why it is so critical to understand fully the terms of any policies you take out. Reading the small print could make a real difference.

Claiming on critical illness cover

Hannah had a combined policy offering both critical illness and life cover. Her husband was covered separately at a significantly higher level, because he was the breadwinner. Hannah had been a very successful art director in TV, but having been made redundant, was running a small business, a charity and doing other ad hoc work. As a result, her income was much lower.

When her ocular melanoma was diagnosed, the critical illness policy paid out a lump sum. However, being the lower income earner, the amount was only small: "We bought a van with the money. It's all we could afford," recalled Hannah. What soon became clear is that as the two policies were linked and, critical illness having paid out, she was left without any cover at all – a serious concern, given the couple have children and a mortgage.

The effects of Hannah's illness

Given the low payout, Hannah was back at work within two weeks. She admits that was a mistake: "It was so hard. I was dealing with trauma, had two kids and was running a household. My charity was all-consuming. But I felt I had to earn an income – we had rent to pay."

The illness triggered Hannah's husband Andy to make a key life decision. Having been running his own post-production company, he felt it was essential that one of them had a stable income. As a result, her husband went back to his old employer, ITV.[7] "He was on a reduced salary, but crucially, he got a pension and excellent critical illness and life cover." With Hannah's lack of cover, the couple saw this as a must-have. Hannah says tongue-in-cheek: "He is really well covered. If one of us was to die, it needs to be him!"

---

7. ITV is a major national TV broadcaster in the UK.

The impact of Covid

Covid was tough for Hannah. Her charity, Mini-Mermaid Running Club, empowers young girls to embrace sport and physical activity as part of their mental health regime. During Covid, her access to schools was cut. She and Andy bought a house in 2020, so had a new mortgage to pay. Ultimately, she too decided to return to an employed role.

Hannah first worked for Leeds Community Foundation and in January 2023 became Corporate Fundraising Manager for St Gemma's Hospice in Leeds. She now has a stable income but remains unable to get critical illness or life cover at an affordable cost.

Hannah's advice to young women

Having experienced first-hand the problems with not saving from a young age, Hannah has very direct advice: "Take out a pension as soon as you start work. If I had taken the final salary pension offered to me by ITV, I would be fine now."

In addition, her challenges with financial protection have taught her a lesson: "Having critical illness and life cover is vital. But do your research and make sure you understand the policies fully. Don't be afraid to ask questions." She knows now that had she had separate policies, she would still have an active life policy, despite her cancers.

Despite her own issues with financial protection, she is still a strong advocate: "I am very physically active, don't drink or smoke. I never thought I would get ill. Many women are told they are superhuman. They are pushed by a narrative that by taking a few supplements they will be healthy forever. In reality, who knows? It's why critical illness and life cover are so important at any age."

Lasting Power of Attorney – LPA

In the UK, a Lasting Power of Attorney (LPA) is a legal document that allows someone (known as the "donor") to appoint one or more individuals (known as "attorneys") to make decisions on their behalf should they become unable to make decisions for themselves in the future.

There are two types of LPAs in the UK:

1. **Property and Financial Affairs LPA:** This LPA allows the appointed attorney(s) to handle the donor's financial and property-related matters. They can manage bank accounts, pay bills, collect benefits, sell property or make investments on behalf of the donor.

2. **Health and Welfare LPA:** This LPA allows the appointed attorney(s) to make decisions regarding the donor's personal welfare, including medical treatment, living arrangements and day-to-day care. It can only be used if the donor loses mental capacity to make these decisions.

There are several reasons why having an LPA is important:

1. **Preparedness for incapacity:** An LPA ensures that if you lose mental capacity due to an accident, illness or old age, someone you trust can step in and manage your affairs on your behalf. Without an LPA, decisions about your finances, property and welfare would need to be made through a lengthy and costly court process.

2. **Personal preferences:** By creating an LPA, you have the opportunity to specify your preferences and instructions regarding your care, treatment and financial matters. This ensures that your attorneys understand your wishes and can make decisions in line with your values and beliefs.

3. **Trusted decision-making:** An LPA allows you to appoint someone you trust as your attorney, such as a family member or close friend, to handle your affairs. It gives you peace of mind, knowing that decisions will be made to protect your best interests.

4. **Avoiding potential disputes:** Having an LPA in place can help prevent disagreements among family members or other interested parties about who should make decisions on your behalf. By appointing attorneys in advance, you provide clarity and reduce the chances of conflicts arising.

LPAs must be created while you have mental capacity. Once you lose capacity, it's too late to create one, and the court may need to appoint a deputy to manage your affairs instead. Therefore, it is advisable to create an LPA as part of your estate planning and to consult with a legal professional to ensure it is drafted correctly and meets your specific needs and circumstances.

WHEN HAVING NO WILL OR POWER OF ATTORNEY CAME CLOSE TO CATASTROPHE

Klementyna's story

Klementyna was faced with not only the stress of her husband being diagnosed with a brain tumour and needing an emergency operation but the realisation that they did not have wills or powers of attorney in place.

Klementyna's husband faced a life-threatening operation after a tumour had been discovered in his brain. They had no will or LPA in place. She had days to get the appropriate documents written and implemented. Here is a story that clearly illustrates why it is so important to have these documents in place, ready for any eventuality.

Finding out your husband has a life-threatening brain tumour while trying to tend to your ten-month-old baby is shocking enough. Imagine, then, not having a will or power of attorney before a potentially fatal operation.

Klementyna's story is a striking example of why having a will and power of attorney in place is essential, whatever your age. You never know when you may need them.

Klementyna met her husband Pawel while studying in Krakow, Poland – her home city (Pawel is originally from Rzeszow). She became a creative copywriter, loving the buzz of advertising in a bohemian city. Pawel studied mechanical engineering (MSc) as well as automation and robotics (BSc), both completed with distinction in 2006. His desire to find the right engineering challenge brought him to England in 2007.

By 2009 they were married and had bought their first house in Braintree, Essex. Over the next five years, the couple developed their careers: Pawel is his own boss at a start-up consultancy specialising in the decontamination of medical devices.

When Pawel decided that the right place for his business was the growing Scottish med-tech scene, they left Braintree and rented in Scotland for nearly six years.

Meanwhile, they began to look for a plot of land around Inverness to build their forever home. In 2017 they found it. After a two-year battle, planning was granted, and as Klementyna says, "Ninety-eight per cent of the neighbours were brilliant." Unfortunately, one made the couple's life a misery. So vitriolic was their opposition to building on the land, that Pawel and Klem's enthusiasm for the project began turning into stress and worry. Still, they were determined to endure. In 2020, as the couple aimed to start a family, Klementyna sadly had a miscarriage. Thankfully she became pregnant again three months later, and in early 2021, their son Hugo was born.

Pawel displays symptoms

It was about that time that Pawel started experiencing fainting episodes. He would occasionally slur his speech and suffer from dizzy spells. His GP diagnosed anxiety and depression and prescribed anti-depression drugs. When he deteriorated, the doctor prescribed a larger dose. Asking repeatedly for a scan proved fruitless.

In February 2022, the concerned couple returned to Poland for a family visit. Half of Pawel's relatives are doctors, and immediately noticed something was wrong. They decided to get Pawel checked and arranged for thorough tests. He had an MRI scan that showed a tumour – an astrocytoma – had consumed half his brain.

With swelling on his brain, Pawel was taken to a specialist hospital in Warsaw to undergo an operation. But that was not the only thing to worry about.

Facing a life-threatening operation with no will or LPA

Doctors made it clear that brain surgery was risky. Turning 40 while in hospital, Pawel could be left without speech or movement or, in the worst case, die. Whilst this was a shocking state of affairs, it had to be considered a genuine possibility. What added to Klementyna's stress was that Pawel had no will or LPA to cover these worst-case scenarios. Having a business, a plot of land and a baby made it essential that both documents were urgently implemented. Without them, Klementyna's ability to manage her husband's welfare, business interests and finances would be seriously limited.

"Pawel was moved to Warsaw for the operation. We had five days to put a will and LPA in place. Luckily, I could do a lot of it online. But being in separate cities did not help." Pawel had his passport, but had left his wallet with his driving licence, National Insurance card and GHIC[8] at the airport to add to the complications.

---

8. The UK Global Health Insurance Card (GHIC) lets you get state healthcare in Europe at a reduced cost or sometimes for free.

A mercy dash managed to retrieve these in time to get the paperwork approved. "I was in survival mode. I had a baby to look after and a deadline to hit. I had to focus on what needed to be done. I could not think about longer-term consequences – I had no control over what could happen anyway."

The aftermath

The operation went well. Pawel woke up, could talk, his memory was intact and he walked the day after. But the treatment was not over – he faced eight weeks of radiotherapy, and in June 2022, he returned to Scotland to start chemotherapy, which concluded in February 2023. Klementyna says: "Chemo was brutal. Pawel is getting stronger every day and is back at his desk, designing. But the recovery of his physical and mental well-being will likely take years." And there are some medications that he will never be able to stop taking, like the anti-seizure pills. Pawel is now in the care of a highly knowledgeable consultant in Aberdeen, making steady progress and has returned to his business full time. As long as the tumour remains dormant, Pawel could live for many years.

The lack of a will and LPA may have caused significant stress, but one thing was taken care of. The couple had a critical illness policy that paid out enough to cover the expenses incurred by the operation and travel to and from Poland. After the diagnosis they also decided to forgo building a house and sold the land, which helped them to buy a new family home in Tain in the Scottish Highlands, without needing a mortgage.

The couple manage their finances well. Both have pensions, critical illness cover and life insurance. Despite this, they lacked two documents that could have proved essential in such a life-threatening situation. Thankfully, Klementyna's calm and methodical approach rectified things in time. Most importantly, Pawel has come through without any of the doomsday scenarios coming to fruition.

Klementyna looks back, knowing how lucky they were: "We were sensible in many ways. But those documents were things we had yet to really consider. I'd tell anyone to make sure you have them. The stress of getting them implemented was a lot, given everything else that was going on. And in a situation like this you want to be able to spend time being with your loved ones, not doing paperwork."

Wills

A will is a vital document and, arguably, the most important that you will make in your lifetime. It provides protection for loved ones and reassurance that your assets will benefit those you intended, not a distant relative you may never have met. Many women shy away from making a will. This is largely because it means facing the inevitable, that you will die someday. However, dying responsibly is a true gift to your family.

The key reasons why you need a will

A will allows you to specify how you want your assets, such as property, money and possessions, to be distributed after your death. Without it, the distribution of your estate will be governed by the rules of intestacy, which may not align with your wishes.

You can appoint executors who will be responsible for administering your estate and ensuring that your wishes are carried out. This can include paying off debts, distributing assets and handling any legal matters. If you don't have a will, the court will appoint an administrator, which may not be someone you would have chosen.

If you have dependent children, a will allows you to appoint guardians who will take care of them in the event of your death. Without one, the court will decide who should be your children's guardian, and it may not be your preferred individual.

A clear and legally valid will can help minimise conflicts and disputes among family members regarding the distribution of your assets. By outlining your wishes explicitly, you can reduce the chances of disagreements and potential legal battles.

A well-drafted will can also help with inheritance tax planning, ensuring your estate is structured in a way that minimises the tax liability for your beneficiaries.

The laws and regulations surrounding wills can vary over time, so it's important to consult with a legal professional or solicitor to ensure that your will is valid and complies with the current legal requirements.

Discussing finances with family

The importance of discussing finances and final wishes with loved ones is often overlooked. It may not be an easy conversation, but it's an important one. Open communication between partners should be encouraged because "knowledge is key".

Subsequently, your will can be structured, aligning your wishes with those of your partner and family. You should consider:

- Who your executors will be
- How you will distribute your estate
- What charities you may want to leave a legacy to.

The structure of a will

This can take various forms and it is not a case of "one size fits all". It's so important that your financial situation is provided in its entirety to your solicitor or will-writer. It is equally crucial that they work in conjunction with your financial advisor to ensure your will is accurately aligned.

You should also consider all of your close family members, particularly those who are financially dependent on you. To avoid any nasty family disputes, it is imperative that you make provision for all of those who you support financially. This can be easily accommodated by the incorporation of a trust in your will, supported by guidance to your trustees in the form of a letter including wishes, alongside an independent professional trustee who will ensure they are carried out. This ensures that grandchildren can't spend the money intended for university on a flashy new car. It also avoids the heartache that can be caused when certain beneficiaries are not accounted for.

Using trusts

The use of trusts in wills is the most flexible way to provide for competing family interests and is widely used in blended family circumstances and also when there is an imbalance in the need for financial support amongst beneficiaries. Will trusts have been used as a way of succession planning and wealth protection for hundreds of years, so they are tried and tested! A common misconception is that they are just for the wealthy, but with the right advice, they can be managed efficiently and cost effectively, providing you with reassurance that your assets will be preserved and protected for your loved ones.

What happens if you die without a will?

If you die without a will, it means you have died "intestate". In such cases, the distribution of your assets and the handling of your estate will be determined by the laws of the jurisdiction in which you reside when you die. Here are some points to consider:

1. Intestate succession: The distribution of your assets will follow a predetermined legal process known as intestate succession. Typically, your spouse and children will be the first in line to inherit your estate. If you don't have a spouse or children, other relatives like parents, siblings or more distant relatives may be entitled to a share.

2. Court appointed administrator: Without a will, the court will appoint an administrator to handle the legal and financial matters of your estate. The administrator will be responsible for settling debts, paying taxes and distributing the assets according to the intestacy laws.

3. Probate process: The lack of a will can result in a more complex and time-consuming probate process. Probate is the legal procedure by which a deceased person's assets are distributed and debts are settled. The court oversees this process to ensure the estate is handled appropriately.

4. Unintended beneficiaries: Intestate succession laws may not align with your personal wishes, leading to assets being distributed differently from how you would have intended. For example, if you are in a long-term relationship but not legally married, your partner will not automatically inherit anything under intestate laws.

5. Increased costs: The absence of a will can potentially lead to higher legal fees and expenses. The probate process may take longer and require more involvement from lawyers and administrators, which can reduce the overall value of your estate.

THE CONSEQUENCES FOR AN UNMARRIED COUPLE WHEN ONE PARTNER DIES WITHOUT A WILL

Faye's story

If I could turn the clock back in my life, it would be to contemplate what cohabiting meant.

I met and fell in love with my partner, who had been married before, and we decided to live together. He didn't want to get married again, he had children from his marriage, and I didn't want any children. So, we agreed I would take his name, and I moved into his house.

I honestly believed there was such a thing as a common-law wife, and despite us not being legally married, I felt like his wife, and he referred to me as such.

We had a fantastic life with lovely holidays and a great social life, and I was able to give up work as he had such a good salary. He decided to retire early as his pension pot was more than enough to sustain us both. The house was paid for, and we enjoyed the finer things in life.

One day he went cycling on his bike, something he loved doing. When he was late back, I wasn't overly concerned, but as the day went on, I became worried.

The doorbell rang, and I thought he had forgotten his key. Imagine my surprise when two policemen were standing there, and they asked if I was his wife, to which of course, I said yes.

The next few minutes passed in a blur as they told me he had died. He had suffered a fatal heart attack, and a passerby had found him on the side of the road.

It was such a shock, and I couldn't take it all in. My friends rallied around me for support and called his grown-up children to inform them. They came straight over. What developed over the next few weeks was nothing short of terrible. He had died without a will. The house was in his name only; all his money and the property was set to go to his surviving children.

We had briefly discussed things a few years before our common-law situation as we saw it. He assumed, as did I, that as we lived together and shared a bank account, I would get the house and any savings, investments and life insurance.

It became clear after his death that this was not the case, as we were not legally married. So, the 15 years we had been together counted for absolutely nothing.

His children wanted to sell the house and asked me to leave; I had no legal right to stay there. I decided to fight and got a lawyer, and, after months, a court case and considerable expense, I gained a settlement which was enough to buy a small house, a far cry from my five-bedroomed home. The worst thing was that the pension died with him, so all that money was lost forever.

His other savings, investments and personal items went to his children, and I had no rights over anything in my home unless I could prove they were mine.

I know for sure this was not what he would have wanted. I accept that we were careless; we made assumptions and didn't plan what would happen if we died. I say "if", because we are all going to die, that is a certainty, so spending a few hours making a will, creating a plan and doing some paperwork is a small sacrifice to ensure your loved ones are cared for.

I advise anyone reading this who is living with a partner, that you have no rights or protection. You must put this in place yourself. Make a will, create a lasting power of attorney, complete the pension paperwork, nominate your beneficiary and ensure the house is in joint names.

Losing the person you love is distressing, but losing your home and being financially worse off makes this so much worse.

Five considerations when making a will

Paula Myers, Director of Legal Services for Private Client Services at Irwin Mitchell Solicitors, shares her advice about making a will. As a solicitor she has dealt with thousands of cases, many of which have proved complex and challenging.

1. Talk openly to your family about your plans for what happens when you die. Share your wishes, such as whether you want to be buried, cremated or donate your body to medical science. You can specify music, favourite poems, a woodland burial, anything that matters to you. This can relieve any potential tension and angst among your family members.

2. Include these plans via a will and a power of attorney. Never assume that what you think will happen, will actually happen, without your express instructions. The power of attorney will be used should you lose capacity.

3. There is no such thing as a common-law wife. You are either a spouse and married, or cohabiting (see more in the section, "The Facts about Cohabiting"). A cohabitee does not have the same legal rights as a spouse. This extends to the intestacy rules and what you expect will happen to a pension on death. The pension trustees have an overall say in this.

4. If you own a business, define who will run the company should you be incapacitated or pass away. Your family members or children might not be the right people for this role for a variety of reasons. So, this needs careful consideration and planning.

5. If you have complicated family arrangements such as blended families or previous marriages, this could create conflict on how an estate is divided up. Talk to everyone involved to explain your wishes. That way everyone will know what to expect when you die. Painful as it may be, deal with conflicting views while you are alive, rather than leaving your family in turmoil.

DEALING WITH THE DEATH OF A LOVED ONE WITH NO WILL

Gemma's story

No one knows when they are going to die. Having a will eases the burden on your family. Not having a will can leave devastating consequences for those left behind, as this story from Gemma, who lost her sister, illustrates.

My sister had just turned 30 when she passed away suddenly, leaving behind two children, a seven-year-old daughter and a son who was just 12 weeks old. Her daughter was from a previous marriage; although she had been separated, she wasn't divorced. She had made a life with a new partner, they had just had their first child and recently got engaged.

In her early 20s, she met her first husband; they married and moved some distance away from us. After getting advice, they bought a house and made this "tenants in common" as she knew that each owner has the right to leave their share of the property to a beneficiary upon their death. She always got advice on big decisions, and although there were conversations about making a will, she felt it wasn't needed as everything would pass to her husband.

After a couple of years, the relationship wasn't working out, so they separated, and they decided to rent the house out; she no longer wanted to live there and wanted to move back to be nearer to us. The rental income covered the mortgage, and they arranged access for their child; the separation was amicable. I assume that the thought of needing a will with this new change in circumstances didn't cross her mind with so much going on.

Eventually, she met someone new, moved in with him and fell pregnant. After the baby was born, she decided she should start divorce proceedings, and she filled in the forms and put them in an envelope with a stamp ready to post.

A few days later, she felt unwell with a headache. Her partner became concerned as her symptoms worsened, so she was rushed to hospital. The doctor suspected a brain haemorrhage, which sadly was confirmed. This was a complete shock; my sister was young, fit and very healthy. She didn't smoke, ate well and led an active life. After placing her on life support, the hospital asked for her next of kin, which was still her husband, as they were still legally married. The hospital finally confirmed the devastating news that there was no brain activity, and we lost my beloved sister. They began to ask her estranged husband questions about organ donation because, as far as they were concerned, he was her next of kin.

In the aftermath of her death, the next subject we discussed was a will. But we discovered she hadn't made one. So, we spoke to her husband and offered to sort out her paperwork and deal with her affairs. They had been separated for four years, so we felt it was our role to sort things out. But he refused in a friendly way, pointing out that it was his job to do this legally. My mum wanted to register her death and organise the funeral. He left her to do this and pay for the funeral. The children were separated to live with their respective fathers. We sorted her personal items, such as clothes and jewellery, but her husband dealt with her bank accounts and financial affairs. We thought he would do the right thing and share the money between the children, but he didn't and kept it. This meant his child benefited, but there was nothing for her son.

If the house had been in joint names, it would have gone to him anyway, but as a "tenant in common" she could have left her half to whomever she wanted. So as there was no will, he inherited the house. We learned that what you expect somebody to do as the right thing differs from what somebody else considers is right.

As a family, we discussed legally challenging the situation as they were heading for divorce, the papers were filled in, they had been separated for so long, and both had moved on. But we felt it could jeopardise our relationship with her daughter and we wanted to maintain contact.

My sister would have been annoyed with herself for not making a will. She had a strong sense of justice, and I'm sure she would have thought her husband would have done the right thing and shared her money equally with her children.

The situation was really difficult. If she had made a will, her husband would not have been able to deal with everything. She probably would have wanted us to fight her husband, but we felt our relationship with her children was far more important. The other thing which surprised us was that he was able to claim widowed parents' allowance because they were still married. So this additional income was also going to him. Had they been divorced, he wouldn't have been allowed to claim that, even if he had custody of their child. This has changed in recent years and has become the bereaved parents' allowance. Her partner got nothing to help raise their child, but this has now changed with this new allowance.

Overall, my message to anyone reading this is that no matter what your age, make a will and review it if your circumstances change. I know my sister would have wished she had, and by me sharing her story, I hope this helps others avoid making that mistake. It's the only way you can ensure who gets a share of your estate and deals with your affairs.

POINTS FOR PROSPERITY

- Do you have critical illness cover?   Yes/No

_____

_____

- Do you have income protection?   Yes/No

_____

_____

- Do you have life insurance?   Yes/No

_____

_____

- Have you written a will?   Yes/No

_____

_____

- Have you implemented an LPA?   Yes/No

_____

_____

If you have answered no to any of the above, please get them in place as soon as you can.

CHAPTER FOUR

Your Money and Your Relationships

"Prosperity is not without many fears and disasters; and adversity is not without comforts and hopes." - Francis Bacon

n the UK almost half of all marriages end in divorce. It is therefore essential you understand and are part of financial decisions. The one person you can rely on is yourself. Don't leave it to chance: if you are in control of your money you will have far more options in life.

Divorce is stressful, and if you don't know your financial situation, this will add another layer of anxiety to the process. This chapter covers the signs of financial abuse, a pernicious development in many relationships today. I also review prenups, postnups, cohabitation and, although I hope it never happens to you, divorce and separation.

The first thing to consider when you are entering into a relationship is: do you share the same financial goals?

THE IMPORTANCE OF SHARED FINANCIAL GOALS

Sapna's story

Life is full of hurdles and Sapna has certainly jumped over a few! Her story highlights the importance of shared financial goals and values with your partner. It also illustrates how life can take unexpected twists and turns.

Sapna's background

My parents taught me financial prudence from a young age. Arriving from Mauritius before my second birthday, they managed to buy a small house and led a frugal lifestyle. "Reduce, Reuse, Recycle" became their mantra before it was trendy.

My parents were doctors, but their attitude to money never changed. I may have been surrounded by children at school whose parents spoiled them, but Dad stayed fixed on his approach: "You can have a car when you can afford to buy one!"

Going to university

Despite my father's desire for me to become an optician, I was determined to study graphic design. And that's what I did, getting onto a fantastic degree course in Newcastle.

After a year of living in halls, buying a property made sense to me. I enlisted five flatmates to cover the mortgage while I lived rent-free on £50 a week.

After graduating, I moved out to live with friends but I kept the house on and rented it out to tenants. It was in my first job that I met my first husband. We moved to Manchester, rented a house together and he proposed.

Our financial challenges

We decided to buy a place together. And that's when the problems started. It emerged he had a CCJ[9] in his name, a barrier no mortgage lender could overcome. I was horrified; he had never mentioned this to me.

When questioned, he said the debt was £1,000, and he was paying off £50 a month. It became apparent our money mindsets were poles apart. He had just spent £200 on Nicole Farhi jumpers rather than prioritising his debts!

I explained I had £1,000 available to pay off the debt, but he said it was *his* debt, and none of my business. I pointed out that it became my business when it stopped us from buying a property.

His financial apathy meant the only way we could buy somewhere was for my parents to act as guarantors. They agreed, but I was mortified to ask them! It transpired the CCJ was for £8,000, not £1,000. I was furious at the deceit. But being young and in love, we carried on planning our wedding.

Months before the wedding, his ex-wife decided she no longer wanted custody of their 11-year-old daughter; she was moving in with her new boyfriend. We were forced to move to a rented house in London. My parents questioned my marriage, but I stayed loyal.

I was 28 and not ready to be a full-time stepmother. The considerable changes in our lives caused significant stress. Working in the media afforded me plenty of opportunities to go out, allowing me to stay out late frequently. It led to us separating for a while.

But of course, love won the day – and we decided to buy a house. I ended up selling the properties in Newcastle (now paid up) and Manchester, so we had a 50 per cent deposit.

---

9. In the UK, someone might have a county court judgment (CCJ) against them if they owe someone money and a court has ruled that they have to pay it back; a CCJ can negatively affect your ability to get credit for up to six years.

But the debt issue had destroyed my trust. We never talked about money. And it meant that we stopped communicating about many other problems.

Once his daughter got a college place, I finally felt I could end things. I paid him a more-than-generous lump sum to buy him out (with the help of my parents), and then we got a DIY "quickie divorce" to save money. I was left with a house and a tiny mortgage and felt financially secure.

Sharing financial goals

Three years later, I met (my now husband) Andy. He was very transparent about his financial situation from the start. We met online, and in our first phone conversation, he revealed that he was in massive debt (much worse than my ex's!).

With my previous experience, that could have been a deal-breaker. But I was financially independent and unconcerned about his situation. Besides, he was so open, honest and in control of his finances, with a payment plan in place, I decided to give him a chance. As a friend said, "You can change the financial situation, but you can't change the character."

Within five months, we were pregnant. I panicked because I thought we couldn't afford this baby yet. But Andy sat me down, popped open an Excel spreadsheet, and we had this amazing, incredibly open conversation about our finances, incomings, outgoings, and how we *could* afford this baby. We worked out that if we cut our cloth accordingly (like my dad taught me to), we'd be OK – and even manage £50 for treats each week!

Of course, we now had a baby on the way; I considered his debt mine too. So, he moved into my house – rent-free, to help pay off his debt quicker (and, of course, to massage my pregnant legs!). I also threw my bonuses from work into the "debt payoff pot" as I was no longer going out partying and getting pricey cabs home!

We married three weeks before our first son was born (due to the imminent birth, it was an intimate affair with just us and our two witnesses).

Life was good. Andy and I started companies to control our time and money.

The difference in having a relationship where I was financially on the same page as my partner was incredible. His responses to critical moments allowed us to deal with many challenges.

In August last year, I was diagnosed with breast cancer. It was a complete shock as we had no family history of cancer and, perhaps arrogantly, I thought my lifestyle was enough. I worked out near-daily, was very fit, ate a good diet, and had no aches, no underlying health conditions.

But Andy's support throughout, including the ability to use his company's private medical insurance policy, made a massive difference to my treatment and recovery.

The future

During lockdown, we introduced a financial advisor who has helped us with pensions and future planning – a decision that delivered us peace of mind.

We already had wills written after my elder son was born. Still, I didn't consider critical illness cover because I'd always been healthy. I thought it unnecessary, given my healthy lifestyle! Now, I cannot get cover.

I hadn't really thought much about retirement as I love what I do, but my advisor helped me amalgamate all my small pension pots from various jobs into one fund. Consequently, I set up a new pension as a self-employed woman.

We bought a new house and moved in early 2023. My mortgage-free property meant we could do a buy-to-let, and we are now renting it out, so it's a brilliant investment for the future.

My advice to young women

Get critical illness cover! You don't think you will need it when you are young, fit and healthy. Until you're not. So, get a policy, along with a will. You never know when you will need them.

And when you choose a partner, ensure they have the same financial attitudes, goals and outlook as you. If they hide any of that stuff from you – run! If you do share the same goals, you should have a relationship built to last.

Financial Abuse

If shared goals are vital, the other end of the spectrum is one partner who controls the other. When one person in a relationship deprives the other from accessing financial resources or deprives them of their ability to earn money, this is known as financial abuse. It is a way for the dominant partner to control the other, ensuring they cannot leave the relationship.

Financial abuse is a genuine issue in the UK. Nearly two out of five adults have experienced it in their current or former relationships, according to a report by The Co-operative Bank and Refuge, the UK's largest domestic abuse charity.[10]

The signs of financial abuse

Financial abuse is commonly carried out by a partner, but this could also be a family member, friend or even a carer. The following list gives some of the signs that you are suffering financial abuse:

---

10. See: https://www.co-operativebank.co.uk/assets/pdf/bank/aboutus/ourbusiness/ Know-Economic-Abuse-Campaign-Press-Release.pdf

- Do you feel you are being restricted from going to work?
- Does your partner make you account for everything you spend your money on?
- Have credit cards and/or loans been taken out in your name without your permission?
- Are your household bills in your name only?
- Is money being spent without you being informed first?
- Have you been forced to hand over control of your accounts?
- Does your partner use your property or take money without your consent?
- Do you have to ask or even beg for money when you need it?
- Are you given a strict allowance and cannot access any more money?
- Does your partner threaten to end the relationship unless you buy them something?
- Have you been stopped from finishing your education?
- Has your partner made threats to evict you if you don't comply with their wishes?

Money problems or financial abuse?

It is important to be clear whether you are facing money issues in your relationship or being subjected to financial abuse. If your partner is genuinely concerned about spending and how much money you have as a couple, that requires open and constructive discussion. It does not necessarily mean that they are trying to control you.

It may be beneficial to designate one of you to manage your finances if the other feels it would positively impact the situation. The key here is that both parties consent to whatever actions are agreed with regards to managing money – even if that results in restricted spending.

However, if you cannot access your money because your partner is "being careful", having had no discussion with you, that is financial abuse. Significantly, uneven resources with one person assuming control of cash allocation is financial abuse.

How to stop financial abuse

Once you recognise you are in a financially abusive relationship, you can do something about it. It may be challenging, but making a clear plan to escape the controls of your partner is essential. Here are steps you should take to make that break:

- **Tell someone.** Getting emotional and practical support from a friend, family member, work colleague or someone you trust is vital in helping you achieve freedom.
- **Gather all your key documents** such as birth certificate, driving licence, passport, marriage certificate, ownership deeds, anything that is material to your identity and your financial situation. Keep them in a secure location away from your partner. Financial abusers are prone to confiscating these types of documents preventing you from getting access to money, property or independence.
- **Find out every asset that is in your name** including mortgage, tenancy agreements, loans, credit cards and any other joint assets you accumulated.
- **Cancel joint bank accounts or credit cards.** This may affect your credit score in the short term but will prevent any increase in debt you cannot otherwise control.
- **Change online passwords** so your partner can no longer access accounts.
- **Open a bank account in your name.**
- **Check your credit report** and look for any adverse history that you are not familiar with.

Financial abuse is a crime

Nobody should have to face domestic abuse, whether it be physical, mental or financial. However, breaking free can seem nigh impossible and terribly daunting for the victim.

It's crucial to remember abuse is a crime not to be taken lightly and is never your fault. If you think you are a victim of financial abuse, use our list above to determine how many signs apply to your relationship. Once you can recognise the problem, you will hopefully find the courage to act. If counselling is not going to resolve the problem, please take steps to get your independence back.

There are some excellent organisations in the UK providing invaluable support to millions of women to extract themselves from abusive relationships and get their lives back. Contact them and get help to take control of your life.

- The Refuge National Domestic Abuse Helpline: 0808 2000 247
- Women's Aid Support: www.womensaid.org.uk
- RCJ Advice: www.rcjadvice.org.uk

OVERCOMING FINANCIAL ABUSE IN A MARRIAGE

Priya's story

Being in a relationship which has shared financial attitudes and goals is vitally important as our next story demonstrates. Priya is a woman who grew up with the right financial habits. But her husband has proved to be terribly undisciplined, getting into substantial debt. He also subjected her to financial and emotional abuse. Priya has done a fine job of taking control of her situation, even though she remains in her marriage.

Priya has been married for over 30 years. For much of that time she has had to scrimp and save to get by, all because her husband was terrible with money. And if she dared to challenge him, he would bombard her with verbal and emotional abuse. Her story demonstrates the pain caused in a relationship where the two partners are at opposite ends of the financial spectrum. She is also a shining example of proving it is possible to take control of your finances, no matter the resistance you face.

Priya's background

Priya grew up in a supportive Indian family who ran their own business. Her parents possessed a wealth mindset. This meant she and her brother were well provided for but were also taught the value of money. She learnt that money should not be wasted, that it is a valuable commodity to be invested and allowed to grow. While still at school she met the boy who would become her husband. She loved this young man and, having left school, the couple decided to marry.

Her mother, being a practical individual, offered her a choice of wedding present: gold or the downpayment on a house. Priya knew exactly what she would choose. She took the downpayment and the couple bought a £60,000 house in Enfield.

When they married in 1991, Priya knew they both needed good jobs to pay their mortgage as rates continued to rise. At the time they were paying around £500 a month.

The new bride got a job in marketing as an administrator while her husband worked in the public sector. What she didn't know, but soon found out, was that he had no interest in money at all. The root of their problems was just beginning.

Moving up the property ladder

After a few years, her husband wanted to move back to his family and friends in Potters Bar. Therefore, the couple decided to rent out their Enfield house. But they couldn't afford to buy in Potters Bar so, as a temporary measure, they moved in with her in-laws. That lasted three years!

Eventually they bought a property in Potters Bar for £135,000, but Priya wasn't happy with the way they went about it: "We sold our house in Enfield to pay for the new one. I would have fought tooth and nail to rent out that house. But he would not have it."

This was one of many examples that demonstrated how far apart they were in terms of financial goals and their attitudes to money.

Divisive financial views

Priya had always been sensible with money. For her, financial security was one of her biggest life goals. Her husband, on the other hand, lived for the moment. Saving and investments were not part of his vocabulary. As their marriage progressed, she began to instigate money conversations with him. Every time she broached the subject, he would become verbally and emotionally abusive. On a couple of occasions, things even got physical. Priya soon put a stop to that by enlisting the help of her brother-in-law. His intervention and her threat to leave if it ever happened again had the desired effect.

What became very clear to her was that she would never get her husband on the same page about money.

Financial secrets

Having moved, Priya took stock of her finances. She had researched saving and investing and realised that the couple had made no progress financially since they'd been married.

They had an arrangement where Priya's husband paid the mortgage and car insurance and she paid for everything else. That meant she had £50 disposable income every month. Luxuries were unthinkable. She realised they had no investments, little savings. He had a pension at work where he contributed just £30 a month and given her wealth mindset, Priya knew they were not doing what was needed to achieve the financial security she so desired.

To make matters worse, Priya's husband remortgaged the house without telling her. Why did he do that? To pay off credit card debt he'd accumulated when she had taken a break from work while having children.

"We had many major arguments about money. When the mortgage statement arrived, it was clear we hadn't moved forward at all," said Priya. Sadly, she added: "After 22 years of marriage, we should have made clear progress. We'd made none."

The penny dropped. "I trusted him too much. I realised no matter how much you love your partner, you can't rely on them. My financial security was down to me and no one else."

An inheritance

The next big development in Priya's story came when her husband's parents died within two years of each other. As a result, he and his brother each inherited half of their estate. They now had £250,000 in the bank. Priya wanted to invest the money. This was a great opportunity to take a significant cash sum and turn it into a much bigger amount. But her husband was not interested. As far as he was concerned it was his money. And all he wanted to do was pay off the mortgage. Given he had remortgaged their house, the settlement left just £15,000 in the bank.

Paying off the mortgage meant her husband was £1,000 a month better off. She waited for him to offer to share the other bills that she had been scrimping and saving to pay for years. The offer never came.

Six months later, she decided to confront him. "It led to a massive argument, but eventually I got my book and a pen and went through our costs to the penny. He hated it!"

Priya got an agreement that the couple would set up a joint bank account to pay for all their household expenses. She told her husband that she would review the bills every six months to ensure they were putting enough in the account. "He couldn't deal with it. I did everything."

Taking control

After 25 years of marriage, Priya finally had help with the household bills and had some disposable income. She started to go out with friends. And she was determined to earn more.

She went into sales, eventually heading up a team (all middle-aged men!). She was so good at her job that her earnings went from £27,000 in 2011 to a £70,000 basic with £25,000 bonuses today. She was totally motivated to be self-reliant and in ten years made it happen.

"I realised if my husband dies tomorrow, he'll leave me with nothing. If I die, he'll get a large death in service payout and the proceeds of my pension. I had to look after myself."

Now she takes holidays and goes out for dinner with friends, can buy clothes when she wants to and has the financial independence she craved for years. That doesn't mean that all her challenges have disappeared.

Planning for the future

Nothing has changed in terms of how Priya and her husband approach money. She is prudent, has a good pension, saves in ISAs and lives within her means. He continues to spend money he doesn't have and has no consideration for the future.

But this spendthrift attitude has caused him problems. "Accumulating credit card debt meant he got a poor credit rating. He drives a big BMW that costs a fortune. I told him to get rid of it, especially as the balloon payment on the contract was a lot of money." But Priya's advice fell on deaf ears: "He just got a loan to pay for it and will be paying it off for another three years."

He also suffers from poor health. "A few years ago, he got a quote for life insurance costing £50 a month. He never went ahead." He is still capable of abuse. When he's particularly annoyed, he'll say: "Don't think you're getting your hands on the

£240,000 I put into the house." This is, of course, irrelevant, given the house is in joint names.

Priya is not worried by these outbursts anymore. "I'm fearless, not angry. I won't tolerate his responses. I won't be held back in life because he can't sort himself out."

For all the issues, Priya is still committed 32 years later. She says: "I love my husband; I still feel a sense of duty. But I feel life is bigger than me and now I am truly empowered. I've gone on a massive personal journey to achieve financial independence, which in turn has brought so many wonderful things."

Last year Priya paid for a family trip to Lake Windermere in a beautiful Airbnb house. As she said: "All my husband had to do was drive us there." She has helped her children, her 30-year-old daughter having married a few years ago and delivered her first grandchild.

Whilst she doesn't think retirement will be as much fun as she had hoped when younger, she has come a long way over the last decade.

What advice does Priya have for women getting into relationships?

Priya was married at 18. She always had a careful and nurturing approach to money. But her husband didn't. Her biggest piece of advice to any woman thinking of marrying or living with a partner is this: "Find out well before you commit what your partner's attitude to money is. Be explicit and very clear about your vision for the future. Make sure you have shared goals that will drive your relationship forward."

It may have taken over 20 years of marriage before something awakened inside her, but Priya has proven that the only person responsible for your financial security is you. She also demonstrates the dangers of not communicating about money early in your relationship. Not doing so can lead to much anguish and stress, and little prosperity.

For some women, they can learn to live with the situation of different financial views and goals, as Priya has. For others, they need to leave and start afresh. When you are young, it can be easy to get into a relationship and, without realising it, eventually become trapped if you are not earning enough money to leave.

Prenuptial Agreements

A prenuptial agreement, more commonly referred to as a prenup, is a legal document that couples may consider before getting married. It is designed to outline how assets and finances should be divided in the event of a separation or divorce.

Here are a few reasons why you might consider putting this document in place before you enter into marriage.

Protect your assets

A prenup allows individuals to protect their pre-marital assets, such as property, investments, businesses or inheritance. It can specify how these assets should be divided in case of a divorce, ensuring that they are not subject to the standard laws of distribution.

Prenuptial agreements can help couples clarify their financial responsibilities and expectations during the marriage. They can outline issues such as financial support, spousal maintenance and division of debts, which can minimise conflicts and provide clarity during a potential separation.

If either party has significant family wealth or wishes to protect family assets, a prenup can help safeguard those assets from being divided or distributed as per the standard laws of divorce. It allows couples to establish clear guidelines on how such assets should be treated in the event of a marital breakdown.

Having a prenuptial agreement can potentially simplify divorce proceedings by pre-determining financial arrangements. This can save time, money and emotional stress that would otherwise be spent on protracted legal battles over asset division.

For some individuals, a prenup provides peace of mind and a sense of security. It offers an opportunity to openly discuss and negotiate financial matters before marriage, ensuring that both parties are on the same page regarding their expectations and protecting their interests.

It's important to note that prenuptial agreements are not automatically legally enforceable in the UK. However, family lawyer Jo Toloczko suggests things you can do to make it more probable that a judge would uphold your wishes:

- Draw up and sign the prenup at least three weeks before you get married. The earlier you both sign the agreement, the more likely a judge will look at it favourably, unconcerned that either party was forced into signing.
- Structure the settlement as close to how a court would view your circumstances as possible. If 95 per cent of all assets are assigned to one party, for example, it is almost certain to be rejected. A 60/40 split is more likely to be upheld, especially if the reasons for doing so are transparent and clearly stated.
- Add a provision for review, typically on the birth of children or after five years.
- Ensure you consult with different solicitors to retain independence.

To ensure the validity and enforceability of a prenuptial agreement, it's advisable to seek independent legal advice from a family law solicitor who can guide you through the process and help draft an agreement that adheres to current legal requirements.

EMBRACING THE FUTURE WITH A PRENUPTIAL AGREEMENT

Gurneet's story

The following story describes a woman's two marriages, one totally unequal, the other, a meeting of minds. She learnt from her mistakes, and second time around, found a man on the same wavelength. He was so aligned with her views, he agreed to enter into a prenuptial agreement when she requested it.

Gurneet is a successful business coach and, now in her mid-30s, she has created her financial independence, working towards true financial security.

But life was not always like this. Gurneet married her first husband when she was only 21, knowing nothing about managing her finances. This was a difficult relationship which ended in divorce, with her walking away with nothing. Her story is one of adversity leading to enlightenment and shows what is possible when a woman consciously decides to take financial control, even having the confidence to put a prenuptial agreement in place before marrying her second husband.

Gurneet's background

Coming from a Sikh family, Gurneet was given no grounding in personal finance. In her culture, men are firmly in control of money matters. "If I asked my mother how much the mortgage payment is, she would say, 'Ask your father'."

When she left home, she admitted, "I had no idea what a bill was." This changed when she went to university and took the first steps to managing her money. After university, Gurneet became a nursery schoolteacher and shortly after this got married.

Married with no financial education

Indian culture treats newly married couples in a nurturing way. The newlyweds live with the husband's parents until they have saved enough to afford a deposit for their own house. Gurneet and her husband were no different, with one exception – her in-laws asked them to pay rent.

At this time her income as a nursery teacher, after paying rent and travel costs, would not leave much for saving for a house deposit.

She was so ignorant about financial issues that she wasn't sure if she was supposed to pay rent individually. "They assured me they were charging rent to us as a couple, not just me." Not knowing what to do, Gurneet turned to the one person she knew could help: her dad. "I called him and told him my in-laws would charge us rent for living there. My dad didn't hesitate. He immediately called my father-in-law and told him that he would take us in if they could not afford to house us."

However, it transpired that the real reason her father-in-law intended to charge rent was not a lack of funds. He explained to her father that he was trying to teach his son some financial responsibility to create stability. Her husband was out of work and needed some motivation to sort himself out.

"Leaving my father to sort this out, so in the end we were not paying any rent, didn't empower me to speak up or walk out," she explained.

She reflects now that she was facing up to three men: her husband, her father-in-law and her dad. It started a process of developing her knowledge and an ability to manage her financial situation.

An unequal marriage

After several years of saving, Gurneet and her husband finally bought their first house. Yet it was Gurneet who saved and paid for the deposit, and she who funded the mortgage payments. "My husband decided he did not want to contribute to the mortgage. By now, he was working in a call centre but didn't want to know about paying half of the mortgage."

Gurneet had learned one very important financial lesson when younger, which was never to default on payments. The fear of CCJs and a permanently damaged credit record kept her awake at night, so she ensured the payments were made.

To do this she took a second job as a waitress: "I'd finish at the nursery, come home, get showered and go out and wait tables four or five nights a week," she recalled. Working two jobs had a damaging impact on her physical and mental well-being. "I was permanently shattered. Ultimately, I lost my job in the nursery because I could barely function."

After much soul-searching, Gurneet felt she needed to leave the marriage. "I left everything behind; I just wanted to get out."

The impact of a marriage break-up

Gurneet was forced to return to her parents' house, leaving her marital home with no car, few clothes and no house. She had no money either, except for the house deposit she had put down. "I had made the stipulation that when we sold the house, the deposit money was mine. We had very little equity because we weren't there for long, but I was keeping that money."

Many may have become bitter at this turn of events, but not Gurneet. "The whole experience made me determined to learn about finance. If I had taken legal advice, I would have got what was rightfully mine from my first marriage."

This led to her consulting with a financial advisor, learning and researching to build her knowledge, and this started to change her life.

Implementing a prenuptial agreement

Gurneet's second serious relationship was moving towards marriage. By now, she was more confident personally and financially. She would not allow a repeat of what happened in her first marriage. "If I was going to get married again, I was going to have a prenuptial agreement to protect my assets."

Starting that conversation with her partner was difficult. "He was taken aback and unsurprisingly kept asking why? But it became a different conversation when I explained in detail what happened through my first marriage and its effect on me."

The couple came to a harmonious conclusion and agreed to get legal advice. They were first told to get individual solicitors to ensure independent advice. The next step was to review what they had individually and as a couple and what they wanted to happen in the worst-case scenario. "It felt like a very open, nurturing conversation." Once they had signed the prenup, the couple never discussed it again. And they are about to buy a property together – their first joint asset. Gurneet looks to the future: "If we choose to have children, it might change again."

Getting a will in place

The prenup is not Gurneet's only consideration: "Nobody thinks about having a will. In my culture, having one is rare, and you hear of so many stories of siblings falling out."

Gurneet drew up her will several years ago and knows having children would require significant changes. She has another key asset that she has built over the last decade – her business. Gurneet is now a business coach, having taken further education. She is helping business leaders manage their companies more effectively whilst creating more balanced home lives. Now in her mid-30s, she is successful in her own right and financially independent.

She has a pension, ISAs, a will and a prenup – a far cry from the 21-year-old woman who married with no idea about personal finance.

Gurneet's advice to young women

"Think about your life at 40 and what finances you'll need. At 21, it feels like a long way off. But it's actually very close."

She admits that she spent every penny when she was younger: "I used to go out every weekend; I'd buy every pair of shoes I wanted." Those days are gone as she has become financially stable. "Now I consider every purchase I make, to the point where people say to me, 'Why do you always think about money?'."

She believes the negative connotations about women wanting to become financially independent must be removed. She likens women and finance to mental health issues. "We're too busy worrying about everyone else and forget about our issues."

Her final advice, which other stories in this book have echoed, is if you are going to get into a permanent relationship, whether married or not, it is essential to have the same attitude to money. "I know too many women stuck in marriages where they are poles apart from their husbands."

Gurneet is a brilliant example of a woman who has overcome a patriarchal culture, a difficult marriage and losing a job to build a successful business and take complete control of her financial situation. It takes guts to tell the man you love you want a prenuptial agreement before marrying him. Gurneet proves that any woman, regardless of background and culture, can be financially successful in life and build a solid foundation if they have the will to do so.

Postnuptial agreements

A postnup works exactly as a prenup with one exception. The agreement is signed at some point after the couple have wed. The same rules apply with the exception of when the agreement is signed. The more reasonable and realistic the structure, the more likely it will be upheld by the court.

The Facts about Cohabiting

Although cohabiting with your nearest and dearest is now the fastest growing "family-type" as opposed to a marriage or civil partnership, it also comes with a few stark warnings that you need to consider.

- You may not have any financial claim in law or a right to financial support from your partner should you separate. You may be able to get extra financial support if you have had a child together, but this is limited. Any top-up will be dependent on whether he is a high earner, or your child has health needs.
- Just because you have lived together for 12 months, or 30 years, does not mean that your relationship will acquire a "formal status" that can be protected if you were to separate. There is no such thing therefore as a "common-law spouse" – it simply does not exist.
- If your partner owns a property in his sole name in which you live and you separate or he dies, you do not have the same "home rights" as you would if you were married or in a civil partnership. Although you may be able to claim a beneficial interest in the property, this can be very difficult to prove and is evidentially based.
- If your partner dies intestate (meaning without leaving a will), you as the surviving partner will not automatically inherit anything from his estate.
- You cannot make a claim against your partner's pension in his lifetime or even upon his death. Assets that pass between you and your partner during your relationship may attract a tax liability which they would not if you were married or in a civil partnership.

Protecting your future

- Draw up clear and effective wills – make sure you know who will get what, should one of you die before the other and do this now.
- Cohabitation agreement – consider drawing up an agreement that confirms who will get what, should you separate, as well as how the structure of your living arrangements will be dealt with whilst you live

together, to include the payment of household bills etc. An agreement can also include "buy out" clauses as well as an agreement as to who should stay in a jointly owned property.

- Get legal structure in place for any property contracts that are drawn up – for example, make sure you have a declaration of trust in place to protect any invested monies you may have put into the purchase of a property.
- Pension planning – get expert advice in this area wherever possible.
- Tax advice – know what needs to be paid and when, so you are not left with a surprisingly large tax bill that you are liable for long after your relationship has ended.

With this insight and advice, you will be better equipped for the unknown future.

Divorce and Separation

Men earn more money than their wives in over 70 per cent of relationships. Women are increasingly principal breadwinners, and nearly three in four work, yet a significant financial disparity exists in earnings and pension savings, an important factor when a couple decides to divorce or separate.

Whilst these life choices are often decided together, invariably, when the relationship breaks down, this financial disparity disadvantages the woman in many ways. In same-sex marriages, the same issue applies where there is an imbalance in earnings and wealth.

This section offers advice about how to protect yourself financially and legally against this most traumatic of events.

Two hugely knowledgeable family and divorce solicitors have shared their expertise.

Carol Grundell has been a divorce lawyer for 25 years. Carol was motivated to become a divorce lawyer following her own protracted and challenging divorce.

Jo Toloczko is a family solicitor at R.W.K. Goodman in the City of London. She has been practising family law for over 30 years, having qualified in 1987.

Dealing with divorce

Divorce is the last resort when a relationship becomes unsalvageable: the more assets and children involved, the more complicated the process.

The divorce process has been made more effortless by the "No Fault" regulations introduced in the Divorce, Dissolution and Separation Act (2020).[11] The changes implemented have removed unnecessary conflict, easing the stress on all concerned. Blame does not need to be apportioned, allowing couples to focus on a financial settlement and, where relevant, the welfare of their children. It also speeds up the process, with a minimum 20-week period introduced between application and conditional order of divorce.

Whilst this has helped immensely, Jo Toloczko advises everyone to get a financial court order:

> *"It is vital to get an order from the court, whatever your financial circumstances. Imagine a scenario where your husband decides at a later date that he deserves a better divorce settlement. Without an order in place, he can renege on the agreement and make an application to the court for financial provision. Ensuring a financial order is implemented during divorce permanently secures your settlement."*

Negotiating a financial settlement

Women should consider several issues before agreeing on the financial outcome of their divorce.

---

11. This Act and the following discussion are relevant to the UK situation. The legal position may be different in other countries.

Jo Toloczko is emphatic about the first:

> *"Never forget about pensions. Many clients say: 'Oh,*
> *it's OK; we'll keep our own pensions.' Yet often, a*
> *husband's pension is highly valuable. It can be worth*
> *more than the marital home. Always review the value*
> *of pensions before deciding how to deal with them."*

Carol Grundell suggests that placing too much value on the home can be harmful:

> *"In my experience, many women (predominantly mothers)*
> *prioritise retaining the family home to provide stability for*
> *the children. Divorce creates such disruption that this becomes*
> *a priority. However, it can often mean receiving less (or none)*
> *of the other assets. It is understandable: a home is a tangible*
> *asset that everybody can comprehend, whereas investments*
> *and pensions can be daunting for someone who doesn't*
> *understand them. Fortunately, the courts and solicitors are*
> *well equipped to deal with this complexity, ensuring equity."*

If you are a mother with young children, not working or on a low income, you may be able to get a court order appropriate to your needs. Do not assume that everything has to be split 50/50. Jo Toloczko says:

> *"There is a principle of sharing and a principle of need.*
> *The latter can trump the former. Suppose one party is more*
> *vulnerable and needs a greater proportion of the financial*
> *settlement to re-house themselves and their children. In*
> *that case, the court will make an award according to*
> *needs. It could be greater than 50 per cent of the assets."*

She has further essential advice: "If your spouse is paying significant spousal or child maintenance, they must have life insurance. You could be in serious financial trouble without cover if anything happens to them. Who pays the premiums can be negotiated between you."

Finally, suppose you own a house as joint tenants, and the divorce is likely to take some time. In that case, you should consider serving a Notice of Severance, converting ownership into tenants in common. This means if you should die during the process, your share of ownership will pass to your preferred beneficiary rather than your former partner. Beware though that this works the other way round too and, if you have become tenants in common and your spouse dies, you could lose out.

Using mediation

Battling a financial settlement through the courts is time-consuming, draining and extremely costly. Mediation is a much better solution, assuming things are not so bad that you can no longer sit in the same room as your former spouse or that they are not acting unreasonably or dishonestly.

The mediation process is well-structured to deliver beneficial outcomes for both parties. The couple undergoes a full disclosure process to ascertain all assets and income to be reviewed. A method to assess options for dividing those assets is then undertaken. Jo Toloczko is a qualified mediator as well as a solicitor and finds the process far better for most couples:

> *"Mediation has a high success rate thanks to the process.*
> *The legal language is removed, which tends to bring*
> *couples together. I can guide and support them towards*
> *settlement, which will cost between £2,000–£3,000 for*
> *the whole process. Going through the courts will cost*
> *four or five times that every time there is a hearing.*
> *It also makes it more likely they will remain friendly*
> *and civil, critical if children are involved."*

Agreeing child arrangements

The courts have taken a back seat regarding children in divorce since The Children Act 1989 came into force. The court will only get involved in child arrangements if it is better for the child if they do so. The onus is, therefore, on the parents to agree on responsibilities amicably.

The Child Maintenance Service (CMS) has made child maintenance more straightforward. It is helpful that the CMS uses a fixed formula to calculate child maintenance. The paying party has to declare their gross income and a percentage is applied for maintenance payments.

Spousal maintenance is less predictable, as the court grants it and does not follow a fixed calculation. If you need additional maintenance from your former spouse, a summary of reasonable monthly budgetary needs will be required. The list will include mortgage or rental payments, utilities, food, travel, etc. The court will assess your income (including child maintenance where relevant) and your expenditure. In many cases, it may order your former partner to contribute toward any shortfall.

Leaving a marriage with little money

Many women remain in unhappy, often dysfunctional, marriages because they have no access to money or experience in managing financial issues. Most of these women have performed the homemaker role. If they divorce, they can no longer afford to stay at home and must re-enter the workforce.

Carol Grundell has seen this many times:

> *"The years spent out of the workforce can have a devastating impact on women's earning potential. Having paused their careers to raise children, they struggle to re-engage in the professional world. If they do, it may be on a low salary. Knowing this, plus depending on their partner for food, housing and other necessities of life, can sway a woman to stay in a marriage that she would much rather leave."*

How does a woman move forward in such conditions, especially when legal fees can prove daunting? Carol Grundell has the following advice:

1. Ask your spouse to pay, given his greater resources. Sadly, this is highly unlikely as most refuse to fund their wife's solicitor.

2. Ask friends or family to help you fund costs in lieu of a final settlement. You can pay them back once the process is completed. Having a solid support network is essential.

3. Take out a commercial litigation loan. This will provide you with the funds you need but is a costly way of acquiring them. It will only work for those expecting a significant sum once their divorce is finalised.

4. Obtain a Legal Services Order (LSO). If your ex-partner refuses to contribute toward your costs, you can ask the court to compel him. An LSO is a costly process, so you may need some help from friends and family to make it happen.

Jo Toloczko also reminds those stuck in a dying marriage that interim maintenance can be applied for. The judge looks at income against monthly costs and makes an early determination whether the spouse should contribute a monthly amount. If your partner is employed, an order is easily enforced. For those with self-employed partners, it can prove more complicated as income figures can be manipulated.

What to do if your spouse refuses to cooperate

In extreme situations, partners refuse to cooperate. That can mean avoiding being served with divorce papers or failing to disclose all financial assets. If you know that your spouse has received the petition, you can apply for a deemed service. If the judge grants the application, it will be deemed that the petition has been served, and the process can continue.

Regarding financial disclosure of assets, this is a compulsory part of the process for both parties. Failure to do so can lead to severe consequences. These can include setting aside the original court order and reviewing the settlement, the judge imposing costs penalties, and parties even being open to fraud charges.

If you believe your spouse is not disclosing all assets, you must urgently discuss your concerns with your solicitor so they can take the necessary action.

Carol Grundell provides a case study where her client had no involvement in the couple's finances and was shocked when her husband asked for a divorce.

I acted for a woman in her 40s, married for 20+ years. Her husband worked in finance in the city, while she had given up her career as a teacher to look after the home and children. She was shocked when her husband told her he wanted a divorce.

When she initially came to see me for advice, she knew nothing about the family's financial position. She truly believed what her husband always told her – that they had no spare money.

From her description of how they had lived for over 20 years, the family had lived a very frugal life. Her husband even told her they didn't have the money to buy GCSE revision books for the children. Knowing what he did for a living, this didn't stack up. On further investigation, millions of pounds invested by the husband were discovered, both in his name and his wife's. (He wasn't best pleased when she changed the password to her online account!)

The wife eventually received a reasonable settlement, but then came the next hurdle.

She didn't have a clue what to do with her newfound wealth. The divorce settlement meant she had a list of actions to arrange:

- Transfer a proportion of her husband's pension into her name.
- Decide where to invest large sums of money.
- Transfer the former matrimonial home into her sole name.
- Ensure she maintained a reasonable income.

Taking such action was an alien world and highly intimidating. I still remember her phoning me when she received her first utility bill. She was in floods of tears, not knowing what to do with it. Her husband had always dealt with these matters.

Naturally, she was advised to seek independent financial advice and, with help, eventually became empowered. Six months later, she phoned me to say how pleased she was with herself. This once blissfully ignorant wife was now in total control of her financial affairs, fully understanding pensions, stocks and shares etc. She even came to enjoy her new financial responsibilities.

I am delighted she improved her situation. However, this is one of many examples I have seen where a lack of financial autonomy or engagement has created terrible problems during and post-divorce.

Women leave themselves financially vulnerable should their marriages fail, simply because they don't understand their household finances. Joint control of family assets prevents husbands from hiding money from their wives. Consequently, the divorce process is made quicker and more straightforward. That ensures the wife's legal and supplementary costs can be kept to affordable levels.

Where the wife has no input, I have seen her give up and accept whatever the husband offers. It has pushed her to her lowest; she simply wanted the process to end. I urge you never to be left in that position.

Five ways to secure a good divorce

I hope this is advice you never have to use. But if you do find yourself going through a divorce, our solicitors have provided five actions you should take. They are as follows:

1. Always obtain a financial court order to secure your settlement.

2. Try different methods of dispute resolution before going to court. It will be cheaper, quicker and less stressful.

3. Never rule out pensions from your settlement.

4. Ensure life insurance and cost-of-living provisions are included in the agreed package.

5. Update your will to ensure your legacy is passed to your chosen beneficiaries.

KEEP CONTROL OF YOUR MONEY

Sarah's story

Sarah's is a case study of a woman not in control of her financial affairs. A negative money mindset, and a husband with terrible financial habits, led to her being financially compromised. I want everyone reading this to take away the clear lesson: do not rely on your partner. Overcome any negative thoughts you have about money and take control!

I began a relationship with my first husband having just left drama school without a single penny and suffering from low self-esteem.

At the time, he worked in the city as a software salesman and had a very high income. We met as I was his tenant, and then we began a relationship. He asked me to marry him, and I got pregnant quite quickly.

Sadly, we lost the baby, but we decided to buy a house and moved halfway between our parents. I qualified as a teacher, which, of course, wasn't a huge salary.

The house we bought was amazing, with lots of land, but it did need work. We had our daughter, but then my husband stopped working due to a back problem. A back problem that continued into another "problem", until I realised he didn't want to work anymore.

I had always thought we were financially stable, but I was shocked to learn that we had no savings or backup. I let him control the finances. Psychologically I think I believed it was his money because I didn't come to the relationship with anything. However, we both agreed I would do the majority of the childcare.

Over time, parcels were being delivered daily. I presumed he had the money to pay for these significant and expensive purchases, but it turned out they were all paid for on credit cards and loans. Shortly after having our second child, we separated, still living in the same house for a while. Subsequently, I moved into my own rental space, and it was then that I realised the full impact of how much debt he had got us into.

I never understood mortgages, but we had remortgaged a couple of times with him asking me to sign various papers. I didn't ask why or comprehend their implications. So, there was no money left from the sale.

He wasn't physically abusive, but I now realise he had been financially abusive from the beginning. He had controlled the finances, and I was kept away from the truth whilst being made to feel guilty that I wasn't paying in as much as he was. Although I now also realise that my teaching salary was much higher than his was because he was only pretending to work.

The split was difficult; there was no money and we were in a massive amount of debt. I had a rented house, which I paid for entirely, and from the moment we split never received any money to bring up our two children. They are both over 18 now and I have paid for everything and still do.

I also now know that he continued taking out credit cards at various addresses and maxed them out. One day the bailiffs turned up at my new house as he had given them the address, trying to claim money for the debts he had accrued. Luckily, I didn't open the door wide enough for them to get in. From that moment on I didn't answer the door for years. I was too scared, and the stress was huge. I only had a humble salary and was financially responsible for everything. Crazy, given it was his debt. Luckily, I got some good advice and proved he didn't live with me, and we were legally separated. He refused to divorce me although eventually had put himself in so much debt he moved abroad. I still pay for everything for our children and even paid for my son to go and see his dad in Thailand so he could have a relationship with him. It wasn't my son's fault it was all such a mess.

When I reflected on how I got into this situation, I realised that my childhood had played a part in my views around money. My parents were working class but decided to send me to a private school. I didn't fit in as my peers were a lot richer and had a lot of "stuff" and expensive holidays etc. There was a real fear from my parents around a lack of money, they were always saying we cannot afford this, and we cannot afford that. It always felt like they struggled financially, and they frequently mentioned they were paying for me to go to private school which made me feel guilty.

So, these mixed messages have led to me suffering from deep anxiety about money, feeling there is never enough.

At 55, I'm still in rented accommodation with my second husband; I have a business but do not have the financial security I crave.

So, my advice to any woman is: take full control of your money from the moment you start work as it's much harder to sort things out the older you get. Financial abuse is so often hidden; if someone is controlling your money then alarm bells should be ringing.

Teaching Your Child about Money

Once you have learned how to control your money, you can teach your children to do the same.

How to handle money is one of the best skills you can teach your children. Showing strength and constraint regarding money and saving for the future will stand them in good stead throughout their lives.

Schools do not teach enough about money skills; as a parent, it is your responsibility. If you ignore this, you risk your children growing up being financially irresponsible and landing themselves into debt and a cycle of financial issues.

So, where do you start?

Here are some ideas on how to help your children be great with money.

Start young

Good habits with money start at a young age.

- Set up a system to earn money for chores and teach them how to save. You can start this from as young as three or four.
- From a young age, teach your children the names of coins and notes and play games that involve money. For example, play being a shopkeeper! Use coins to draw around and to make patterns and designs!
- Teach your children about "want versus need" – an important concept to learn in life. For example, they might want the latest toy but discuss how they can purchase this. It could be using birthday money or savings, but also raise the subject as to whether there is a less costly alternative.
- With birthday and Christmas money, always save at least half. Put this in an account where they can see it grow. For example, if they saved £100 every Christmas and birthday, by the time they were 18 they would have at least £1,800 (could be more, depending on where it was invested). Quite a little nest egg, which could go towards driving lessons or their first car.
- Teach your children that they cannot have everything they want. Setting boundaries at an early age will reap rewards later.

Tweenagers to adulthood

Once your child is around 9–12, they can quickly begin to learn the pricing and value of goods and services.

- For example, when going out for a meal, discuss pricing.
- Talk about the items they are saving for and where they can look for price comparisons.
- Get them familiar with the concept of checking for the best price for an item or the best deal in a restaurant.
- As your child reaches their teenage years, open an account with a debit card so they can start to learn how to manage money online. Then by the time they are working part time, this process is familiar to them.
- It is essential to work with your child before they go off to university and teach them budgeting for food, utility bills and rent. Take your children food shopping so they know and understand prices and how to shop for the best deals.

Being honest

Lack of money can be a source of shame and embarrassment for many parents. If your children are aware of your financial situation, they will then start to understand.

Saying no to your children is OK!

Transparency is important.

Hiding the problem if times are tough is not the answer. A careful explanation will gain respect from your children. You do not have to share specific numbers, just an overview and a sense of where you are financially.

Share the basics of what you can and cannot afford but avoid using the word afford.

A good expression is to say, "we choose to spend our money on this instead". Children then understand there are always financial limits in life. This is not about burdening your children with financial woes but encouraging open and honest conversations.

Plan your children's financial future with them. Talk about saving for university, driving lessons, a car and first house. Share your experiences and ideas with them. Discuss pensions and investments and how money can grow, and give them a copy of this book!

POINTS FOR PROSPERITY

Review your financial goals with your partner. Are they in sync? Are you actively helping your children understand how to manage money?

_____

_____

_____

_____

_____

Do you see signs of financial abuse in your relationship?

If yes, get help. There are some wonderful organisations listed on page 107 and do check for organisations locally to you.

_____

_____

_____

_____

_____

Do you need a pre- or postnup?

_____

_____

_____

_____

If you are cohabiting, have you protected yourself?

If no, what action will you take next?

_____

_____

_____

_____

CHAPTER FIVE

Business Finances

"Just try new things. Don't be afraid. Step out of your comfort zones and soar." - Michelle Obama

This chapter is for anyone who is thinking of starting a business or has their own business or a side hustle.

Running Your Own Business

I asked accountant Andrea Richards, founder of Accounts Navigator, to share some important considerations when running your business – here is her checklist of what you need to consider:

☐ **Register with HMRC.** If you're freelancing, running a side hustle or setting up your own business, you must register as self-employed with His Majesty's Revenue and Customs (HMRC). You can register online through the HMRC website or by calling their helpline. You must do this as soon as possible, but legally, you must register by 5 October after the end of the tax year in which you became self-employed.

☐ **Decide on the legal structure.** There are different legal structures for businesses, including a partnership, limited companies (Ltd) and self-employment, generally known as a sole trader. Each structure has its advantages and considerations. Discuss with an accountant the best set-up for you.

☐ **National Insurance.** As a self-employed individual, you're responsible for paying income tax and Class 2 and Class 4 National Insurance contributions. Class 2 contributions are a flat weekly rate, while Class 4 contributions are based on your profits. You may be eligible for certain exemptions or reduced rates, so it's advisable to check with HMRC or an accountant.

☐ **Keep accurate records.** Record your income and expenses related to your freelance or side-hustle activities. This includes invoices, receipts and bank statements. These records will be necessary for completing your self-assessment tax return. You can use a spreadsheet or cloud accounting systems like Xero, Sage or QuickBooks.

☐ **Allowable expenses.** You can deduct expenses incurred for your business, freelancing or side hustle when calculating your taxable profit. These may include costs for equipment, supplies, travel, marketing and professional fees. It's essential to keep records of these expenses and ensure they are solely for business purposes. HMRC has a list on their website of allowable expenses.

☐ **Self-assessment tax return.** You must complete a tax return each year, reporting your income and expenses from your freelancing or side hustle. The deadline for filing is usually 31 January, following the end of the tax year (5 April). You can file online using the HMRC website or seek assistance from an accountant.

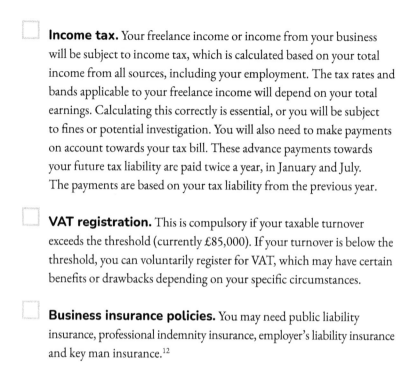

Income tax. Your freelance income or income from your business will be subject to income tax, which is calculated based on your total income from all sources, including your employment. The tax rates and bands applicable to your freelance income will depend on your total earnings. Calculating this correctly is essential, or you will be subject to fines or potential investigation. You will also need to make payments on account towards your tax bill. These advance payments towards your future tax liability are paid twice a year, in January and July. The payments are based on your tax liability from the previous year.

VAT registration. This is compulsory if your taxable turnover exceeds the threshold (currently £85,000). If your turnover is below the threshold, you can voluntarily register for VAT, which may have certain benefits or drawbacks depending on your specific circumstances.

Business insurance policies. You may need public liability insurance, professional indemnity insurance, employer's liability insurance and key man insurance.[12]

Reducing Your Tax Liability

Andrea advises to work with an accountant who can help you take advantage of tax-free allowances and reliefs provided by HMRC. Ensure that you maximise your personal allowance, the income you can earn tax free each year. Additionally, use tax reliefs such as the marriage allowance, which allows couples to transfer a portion of their personal allowance to their partner if they meet certain eligibility criteria.

---

12. Key man insurance or key person insurance refers to insurance policies that protect businesses from the loss of a key individual who is unable to work due to a critical or terminal illness, or has passed away during the length of a policy.

If you decide to open a limited company as a limited company director, you have more flexibility in how you pay yourself. By effectively structuring your salary and dividends, you can minimise your overall tax liability. Discuss with an accountant how best to do this.

There are tax benefits to contributing to a pension as these contributions are eligible for tax relief, meaning you receive tax relief on the amount you contribute, subject to certain thresholds.

Capital gains tax (CGT)[13] applies if you have assets that have increased in value, such as property, shares or investments; you may be liable for capital gains tax when you sell them. However, there are various exemptions and reliefs available that can help reduce your CGT liability. For instance, you can utilise your annual CGT allowance, consider transferring assets to your spouse or civil partner, or explore tax-efficient investment options like Venture Capital Trusts (VCTs).

Freelancing/Side hustles

Freelancing or having a side hustle while employed is common for many individuals; it can be great for increasing your monthly income.

Whether freelancing, selling crafts or providing services, understanding the rules and regulations surrounding your side gig is essential.

If your side hustle brings in earnings surpassing the £1,000 threshold, it is mandatory to declare your income on your self-assessment tax return. Income below £1,000 doesn't need to be declared.

---

13. Capital Gains Tax is applicable in the UK, and the advice here is relevant for the UK only. Please be aware that tax rules in other countries may be different.

Beware of Scams!

Get-rich-quick schemes are in abundance. I would be very wary of anyone promising you high-income returns on investments, selling schemes or anything else which seems too good to be true.

Often people get involved in selling products for a commission; in most cases, the only people making money are the company. If you must invest money in starter kits and are expected to sell to friends and family, be warned! This will probably leave you worse off.

Cryptocurrency schemes are also doing the rounds, and these schemes are sophisticated and can trick you into believing friends and family have taken this up. Just be careful, and don't be sucked in with the promise of making money quickly.

Legitimate investment schemes will be FCA regulated[14] and, if in doubt, seek advice from a professional such as a financial advisor or qualified accountant.

Protecting Your Business

If you already own your business, I urge you to consider what will happen if you are sick and cannot run your business. How would the business function without you? What should happen to your business in the event of your death?

If you have partners in your business, how will they be impacted?

Consider taking out a key man insurance policy, as this helps to ensure the business can absorb the strain of losing critical people in the business.

---

14. The Financial Conduct Authority (FCA) is a financial regulatory body in the United Kingdom which operates independently of the UK Government.

The business is separate from your personal finances, so you need to review your situation and work out how best to cover the company.

Define what will happen to your business in your lasting power of attorney and will.

Unless proper arrangements are made, shares of a business will go to the next of kin. So, for example, if you have a business with a female partner and she dies, her husband will inherit her shares. So, if you want your shares to go to someone else on death, you must state this in your will.

Agreements

If you are in partnership with someone, make sure you have a partnership agreement so you are clear about what would happen if one of you dies or can no longer work. A limited company with multiple directors needs a shareholders' agreement.

Every time people are told they need an agreement, it suggests a lack of trust, when you're actually trying to create security for everybody involved. Any contract ensures that both parties are looked after, and responsibilities are defined. That doesn't mean you don't trust each other. It just means that everything is in place to ensure everyone's OK if anything changes.

Always remember that an agreement is an insurance policy. It isn't about a lack of trust but about enforcing the structure you've set up. Things go wrong when there are no agreements, because people have accidents and die. People get ill and cannot work, so having conversations at the start of a business saves problems later.

Get help building your business from your local enterprise agency or networking groups and look at working with a business coach.

Running a business isn't for everyone, so think and carefully consider the implications of becoming self-employed and understand the risk involved. Advice from professionals to help you understand all the aspects of owning your own business is vital.

POINTS FOR PROSPERITY

- Make sure you are registered with HMRC and understand your responsibilities.

_____

_____

- Have you got your business fully covered?

_____

_____

- Gain help to grow and progress your business.

_____

_____

CHAPTER SIX

Creating a Prosperous Mindset

"A positive attitude is essential on the journey to prosperity." - Diane Watson

want you to be an empowered woman thriving financially and in life. When I look at the most successful people, they have one thing that stands out: a positive mindset. Eradicating negative thoughts and building a positive mentality is one of the essential building blocks of success.

This is certainly true for anyone aiming to create financial independence and security. Every woman needs to develop a prosperous mindset if they want to achieve their financial goals. Firstly, it makes you believe you deserve prosperity. Once you embed that belief, you can create positive habits that will help you towards building wealth.

This section will explain how your attitudes to money were formed. It doesn't matter if those attitudes are positive or negative at this stage. The key is to recognise what has formed them.

With greater understanding, you can begin to adjust your money mindset. I have enlisted the help of a top NLP[15] coach, Amanda Foo-Ryland, to offer you a process for creating a prosperous mindset.

By the end of this chapter, you should have the tools and knowledge to build the most positive mentality toward money.

How Your Background and Childhood Influence Your Relationship with Money

I have worked with thousands of people over my 30-year career as a financial advisor and it's very clear that childhood experiences play a significant role in shaping an individual's attitudes, beliefs and behaviours related to money.

The circumstances surrounding your childhood hugely influence your relationship with money. Here are some reasons for this.

- **Your parental influence.** The way parents or caregivers handle money and financial discussions can leave a lasting impression on children. If your parents were frugal and responsible with money, you are more likely to adopt similar habits. On the other hand, if your parents were irresponsible or had a scarcity mindset, you might have developed negative beliefs around money. Of course, this can also have the opposite effect. So, if you were brought up in an environment of lack, as soon as you get your own money you might become a spender.
- **Socioeconomic background.** The socioeconomic background you grow up in can impact your perception of money. Children from financially stable households may develop a sense of security and

---

15. Neuro Linguistic Programming is commonly referred to as NLP.

confidence around money, while those from low-income families might develop a scarcity mindset or feel anxious about financial matters.

- **Financial education.** The level of financial education received during childhood can influence how you manage money as an adult. If children are taught the value of saving, budgeting and investing, they are more likely to make informed financial decisions later in life.
- **Money messages.** Messages conveyed by parents or influential figures during childhood, such as "money is the root of all evil" or "money can't buy happiness", can shape a person's beliefs about money and wealth.
- **Emotional associations.** Positive or negative emotional experiences related to money during childhood can affect one's relationship with money in adulthood. For example, being rewarded for good behaviour with money might create positive associations, while witnessing financial struggles or conflicts can lead to negative associations.
- **Role models.** Children often look up to adults as role models. Observing how adults handle money, whether responsibly or impulsively, can influence their own financial behaviour.
- **Traumatic financial events.** Experiencing significant financial hardships during childhood, such as witnessing bankruptcy or debt problems, can create deep-rooted fears and anxieties about money.

It's essential to recognise how childhood experiences have impacted your relationship with money to better understand your financial behaviours and make positive changes if needed. With self-awareness and a willingness to learn, you can develop a healthier and more balanced attitude towards money.

Improving Your Money Mindset

Over the course of my career as a financial advisor, I have had so many conversations with people who believe they are "no good" with money.

With the right help and support, anyone can improve their relationship with money and work towards creating a positive financial future.

I spoke to Dr Amanda Foo-Ryland, an NLP trainer and an expert in neurology, who works with people to help them erase limiting beliefs that don't serve them, installing new ones that do. Here are her thoughts about how we develop limiting beliefs and what we can do to break them down.

How are limiting beliefs installed?

We know that attitudes around money are established very early on in our lives, and these play out when we are responsible for our money behaviour.

Up to the age of seven children are learning machines and they operate in a hypnotic state. Their brains function in Theta, allowing them to absorb so much information.[16] They are literally little sponges. There is no conscious mind or brain functioning at Beta level, our conscious mind's way of operating.[17] It is a structure that allows the child to absorb everything from their environment.

The child treats everything as truth; they are incapable of objectivity and unable to disagree, as there's no logical thinking until the age of seven.

If a child is exposed to parents who have poor money habits such as gambling or a spending addiction, this can create an unhealthy relationship with money. Being raised in poverty or wealth can also distort beliefs around money. The first stage is to step back to understand where your financial beliefs stem from. Once you have reflected, then you can work on creating new behaviours.

If talking about money or dealing with finances creates anxiety and worry for you, then reflect on what causes these feelings for you.

---

16. The brain tends to produce theta waves during sleeping or dreaming. Theta brain waves can also occur when you're awake and in a very deeply relaxed state of mind.
17. Beta waves are high-frequency, low-amplitude brain waves that are commonly observed in an awake state. They are involved in conscious thought and logical thinking.

Amanda has developed the 'Sherlock Holmes' process to help her clients uncover their limiting beliefs.

Here is what you need to do:

To do this properly, select a time during your "normal" life, working or at home, and in your regular routine. Avoid a time when you are away or something out of the ordinary is happening. When you are ready, follow the process below.

Over the next 48 hours, catch yourself every time you have a negative thought about money. Stop, and, where possible, move yourself from the space in which you had the negative thought. For example, if you were sitting at your desk when you had that thought, stand up and move away from the desk and stand to the side of it.

Now get your "Sherlock Holmes" on.

At this point, you are outside of yourself. You become Sherlock Holmes, the great detective, investigating your thoughts. You are going to ask the person sitting at your desk this question:

"What is it that [insert your name] believes about themselves that caused them to think that?"

So, if I were running this process, wanting to discover the deepest unknown, I would recognise the negative thought, stand up and move to the side and say:

"What is it that Amanda believes about herself that caused her to think that?"

And I would wait. Then there will be some great feedback; our brain is designed to answer questions, and the question's quality will determine the answer's quality.

By following this process, you also create a pattern interrupt where you become conscious of the programme that runs unconsciously.

Being aware of it gives us immense power because we can now interrupt that pattern. It can't fly underneath the radar any longer; it's almost like we have outed it.

You can consciously say to our unconscious self, "No, sorry, we're not running your programme. So, stop right there."

The programme that normally takes a negative thought and converts it into behaviour (as we know, thoughts become things), is now halted; it cannot run its normal path.

In financial terms, negative thoughts lead to sabotaging behaviour such as overspending, failing to explore positive investment opportunities, punishing yourself with a cycle of negative narratives, saying no to things you know you would enjoy, and feeling uncomfortable with wealth.

The pattern interrupt means you will get a better outcome while running this programme, but it is not permanent and is only effective whilst you act as your own Sherlock Holmes.

This is how we uncover the most profound unknowns by observing and listening to what our neurology reveals. You can then work on deleting these thoughts and working on new behaviour patterns.

Once you understand where your issues with money began, I advise you to work on understanding how your finances should be working. If you have any spending addiction or gambling problems, seek expert help.

I have seen hundreds of people improve their relationship with money simply by becoming more knowledgeable.

Knowledge is power. Educate yourself and take time to understand personal finance and money; the fact you're reading this book is a great start.

- Please do not listen to your friends' opinions about financial matters at the pub; they are not experts!
- Learn about the impact of inflation on your savings.
- Understand the power of compound interest.
- Set your financial goals and plan how you will achieve them. You must work on looking at the bigger picture and understanding the risks you face for not making the right financial choices.

The phrase, "a man is not a financial plan", is a common saying that highlights the importance of financial independence and responsibility. It emphasises that there are better approaches to managing your finances than relying solely on a romantic partner for financial security.

As we have shared in this book, relationships can be unpredictable, therefore, you must be in control of your money; be responsible for yourself.

Women have often been made to feel they were not good at maths at school, which has translated into poor money habits leading them to bury their heads in the sand. Many women I have worked with have abdicated responsibility for their finances to their partners, often using the excuse that it's too difficult to learn how to manage money.

In some cases, a person's relationship with money is damaged, but it is never broken beyond repair. It can be healed with support. I have seen this happen many times. As a financial advisor nothing gives me greater pleasure than working with someone who has a newfound confidence around money.

Develop Positive Habits

Admitting you have an issue with money is the first step to dealing with the problem. It requires patience, discipline and a willingness to adapt to changing your spending habits.

Avoid impulsive spending and learn financial discipline. Delay gratification and consider your purchases. Be mindful of emotional spending and work on coping with stress or boredom without spending money.

Improving your relationship with money is crucial to achieving financial well-being and overall happiness. Avoid comparing yourself to others, as everyone's circumstances are different. Focus your mind on you!

Taking proactive steps and being mindful of your financial decisions can cultivate a healthier and more positive relationship with money over time. And it will make a positive impact on your mental health.

TURNING YOUR LIFE AROUND

Louise's story

Our last story in this section covers a long painful journey into addiction, debt and abusive relationships. This is a positive story which shows what can be achieved and how you can turn your life around.

Louise's life was a rollercoaster ride of materialism, over-indulgence, addiction and abuse. But having lost everything, she put herself through recovery and counselling and found a new purpose: to help others. Financially, her experience has taught her hard lessons yet provided the foundations for a completely different approach to money. One that looks to the long term, not living for the moment.

Louise's background

Louise's father worked extremely hard; he set up his own successful printing business. She was one of three children and had a very comfortable childhood. Looking back, she felt that her parents used money as a form of affection rather than giving it physically. This was the root of her negative money mindset.

She was clever and went to university, resulting in the opportunity to work for a property development company while she completed her degree.

After graduating, her first job paid £18,000 a year and a company car, a reasonable salary at the turn of the millennium.

Spending out of control

The property world around 20 years ago was made for those who liked luxury and there was a lot of money being spent. Louise got the bug almost immediately. She says, "I was working in the property market during boom time. I became very materialistic and just wanted more shiny things. I had my first flat at 22, had my company car, and spent money like nobody's business." She admits that the people around her were extravagant and would think nothing of hiring helicopters or going to the most expensive restaurants. "I was soon overspending, racking up significant credit card debt."

Looking back now, she realises she saw money as validation, a symptom of her negative mindset. "I thought it presented to people how good you were."

Several years later, she met the father of her son, and they eventually married. They also set up a buy-to-let business, leading to an even greater spending spree, buying a house worth more than £1 million. "It was so easy to get money at that time."

Being in a controlling relationship

Unfortunately, the marriage and business did not last. She says, "I went into another relationship and had another child but still had not got any control on my spending and I was going from one relationship to another. After suffering with postnatal depression my life began spiralling out of control. I frittered away money and was struggling financially. To make matters worse, I then got into a violent controlling relationship and developed a problem with alcoholic dependency."

This new relationship was the result of an introduction just before the pandemic hit. "I didn't spot the signs and as the Covid lockdown started, he moved in. He started 'love bombing' me. If I'm honest, I quite enjoyed it. It made me feel good that somebody wanted to be with me. I was blind to some red flags. I ignored things. For example, how quickly he had supposedly fallen in love with me, how he took control of my finances, the way he cut me off from my family. This led to 18 months of increasing control and violence. It became apparent that he was a drug addict and I had slid into alcohol addiction. He took complete control of my life, convincing me I didn't have an issue with alcohol, regularly buying me drink. Looking back, I think it was easy for him to control me when I was drunk all the time."

"He was extremely jealous, stopping anyone from talking to me and became increasingly manipulative and violent. In 2021, I reached my lowest ebb. I felt we were unsafe in the house, so I fled to my parents while my children were sent elsewhere. I left with nothing. He had taken all my confidence."

Things couldn't get much worse. The time had come to get her life back on track.

The road to recovery

Once Louise had reached safety, she started a recovery programme with a specialist at Women's Health Matters, a charity organisation which helps survivors of domestic abuse. She undertook a 28-week course, helping to identify red flags, stop recurring patterns of behaviour and learn to forgive herself. Through

Women's Health Matters Louise met a representative from Smart Works Leeds, a charity that dresses and coaches unemployed women for interview and job success.

They helped her succeed at an interview, which resulted in a "game changing" job with a partnership made up of specialists from community charities and the NHS Trust assisting people with addiction. Louise now has a purpose.

Regaining financial control

The changes in Louise's life are a seismic shift from where she was: "I look at money completely differently now. It really hurt losing everything, but I had to accept it. I now write down everything I spend, budget weekly and stick to it. Instead of buying designer clothes, I get a buzz in finding a bargain on Vinted!"[18]

There is one other issue that has complicated things. Having come through a destructive relationship and beaten alcoholism, Louise has been diagnosed with breast cancer. She had an operation and was due to start radiotherapy at the time of writing. Thankfully, her prognosis is excellent, but life insurance is now unavailable. However, she has been sensible and ensured her will is written.

As her children get older, she aims to instil her newfound discipline in them. Not surprisingly, she wants them to avoid the mistakes she made in her 20s and 30s.

Louise's advice to young women

Louise is adamant: "Keep your head down. Don't get your head turned by any man." While finding the right relationship and taking control of your own life is essential, she also talks about the long term. "Build yourself a foundation. If you have a career, stick to it. Please don't do what I did and throw away a great

---

18. Vinted is an app for selling and buying second-hand clothes and other items.

job. Think about longevity. It doesn't seem to matter when you're in your 20s, but it is so important."

Louise has long since stopped believing in the adage, "live for the moment". "I absolutely believe you have to make a plan for the future. I want to show my children that planning for the future leads to security and happiness." She doesn't think everybody should stop enjoying their lives but recognises that balance is everything.

Louise has witnessed the extremes of life. She has had a statement house, big cars, taken amazing holidays. But destructive relationships and alcohol took them away. She has learnt tough lessons, but today proves that you can create a positive mindset to improve your relationship with money at any time in your life. And it's always possible to get your finances back on track.

POINTS FOR PROSPERITY

Define your beliefs about money.

_____

_____

_____

_____

Did you need a Sherlock Holmes investigation?

If so, what did you discover?

_____

_____

_____

_____

Set three priorities for creating a positive money mindset.

1. _____

2. _____

3. _____

CHAPTER SEVEN

You Can Prosper

*"There are many roads to prosperity,
my advice is taking the road to action as
inaction leads nowhere!"* - Diane Watson

P revious sections have hopefully given you the tools and a much clearer understanding to start your journey to financial independence. This chapter explains why you should use a financial advisor to help you on your way.

If you have avoided using an advisor in the past, nervous they will judge you, ask for information you don't know or cost you money you cannot afford, let me dispel the myths. I will help you find the right advisor and tell you how they work, what you need to know and why you need one.

Working with a Financial Advisor

My job as a financial advisor is to help clients achieve their financial goals. I help them make informed decisions, by understanding their current financial position, filling in gaps and assessing their options. A good financial advisor should be able to eliminate jargon and tell you what you need to know in comprehensible terms. They will also challenge you if you say one thing and do another.

As with any professional consultation, you can expect to go through a well-designed framework for reviewing your financial status. The financial sector is heavily regulated, and you can expect a professional approach that delivers outcomes right for you and your future goals.

This section covers the typical questions you may ask before deciding to consult an advisor.

How do you find a financial advisor?

You can find a good financial advisor through recommendations from friends or family. Or check online and then read their online reviews.

Recommendations on sites such as VouchedFor, Trustpilot and LinkedIn and Google reviews are a good place to check. Make sure they are registered with the Financial Conduct Authority – www.fca.org.uk.

Why do you need a financial advisor?

Here are some examples of the types of advice financial advisors deal with:

1. A customer has worked for several employers and has pensions with each. They have no idea what their retirement pot looks like and what to do with it.

2. Having reviewed their pension funds, a client is concerned there is a shortfall between their target retirement pot and their current projected total.

3. A customer has little understanding of how and where to invest spare cash.

4. Investment needs have changed and an individual needs help in finding the right strategy.

5. People do not comprehend the different financial packages on the market, and which are best for them.

6. An event occurs that makes a client realise their need for financial protection.

7. There has been a life event. This could be a birth, death, divorce, house move or even a lottery win!

What information do you need to provide when meeting a financial advisor?

The first thing to do is create a schedule of all your pensions. Provide suppliers, account numbers and the last statement fund value if possible.

If you have a mortgage, confirm your provider and the current outstanding balance.

Once you have that, outline any protection you have, i.e. life insurance and what it pays out, critical illness or income protection policies.

It would also be useful if you considered:

- When you want to retire
- How much you want in your retirement fund
- What savings you have and what returns you are getting
- Your attitude to risk – this affects the types of investments that may be right for you.

How long is an initial meeting?

Unless there are particular complications, a typical first meeting lasts about an hour. It is quite relaxed; the advisor's job is to get to know you and collate the required information to complete a comprehensive financial review for you. After that, you can decide if that advisor is someone you want to work with.

What happens next?

Following the meeting, the advisor will often have a lot of work to do to research your products in more detail. This will allow them to complete the review and identify concerns and gaps in the customer portfolio.

For example, every customer is asked if they have a will. If not, they will almost certainly be advised to get one. Most advisors have trusted partners who are professional will writers, even if they do not offer the service themselves.

If you run a business, this will require additional attention. Consider:

- Do you have income protection?
- Does your will (if you have one) reflect what should happen if you were to die or be incapacitated?

The pension funds are reviewed, including costs, performance and options for alternative investments.

An advisor will help you decide if it is right to consolidate multiple pension funds into one or whether your different accounts can meet your needs.

Most importantly, they will tell you what you are projected to receive on retirement against where you want to be. If there is a deficit, they will talk to you about what can be done to reduce it.

You should receive a cash-flow model that illustrates your income and expenditure and what would happen if you couldn't work for specific periods of time. That helps you understand whether you could manage on a reduced income and the impact it would have on your pension savings.

If you have an interest-only mortgage, your advisor will talk to you about how you intend to pay it off at the end of the agreement.

Do you have to pay a financial advisor?

Given you will be employing a professional consultant, there are costs involved. Often, their fees are incorporated into your financial products. They will declare what these are and how much will be included in your product charges, so you know exactly where you stand. They will also declare how much commission they will earn if they introduce new products to you.

Keeping in touch

A financial advisor must carry out an annual review with you (this is an FCA regulation) to monitor your financial position and update any changes in your life.

They will continue to ask you if your financial goals have changed: do you want to retire earlier, do you need more money, do you want to increase your investments and more?

THE BENEFITS OF WORKING WITH A FINANCIAL ADVISOR FROM A YOUNG AGE

Vicky's story

The following story highlights Vicky, a successful optician running her own business with her husband. She first used a financial advisor when she left university and has never looked back. Now in her 50s, her finances are in good health, and she is on track to achieve both her financial and life goals.

Vicky first consulted a financial advisor, aged 21, when she qualified as an optician. Since then, she has used them to make critical decisions throughout her adult life. By doing so, she has put robust protection in place for her family and is in a healthy financial position. Her story highlights how her goal to achieve financial security should see Vicky and her husband live a happy and comfortable retirement.

Vicky's background

Vicky has been heavily influenced by her early years. Her parents divorced when she was just two years old. Her mum did not work, allowing her father to dictate terms.

Unsurprisingly, he would not fund a solicitor for her mum to fight the settlement, so she was left in a poor financial state: "Things were so bad, mum couldn't afford cleaning products", Vicky recalled.

Things got better when her mother met Vicky's future stepfather. They married, and the family moved to London. Yet her mother repeated the pattern of reliance on her second husband, who was the sole breadwinner.

As Vicky got older, these events shaped her attitude toward money. Her mother's inability to control her financial situation left Vicky determined never to rely on a man for her financial security.

Her dad and stepfather encouraged this attitude, getting her to save from her early years, supporting her desire to be financially in control.

Using a financial advisor from a young age

Vicky went to Cardiff University to study optometry. She qualified, left home and her stepdad introduced her to a financial advisor. She started to build a savings pot for her future and any unexpected expenditure. Here was a woman focused on her financial security, creating a pension aged 21.

While studying at university, the young optometrist met her husband, who subsequently became her business partner too. The optometrists bought into their current business in 2005, retaining a 50 per cent stake today, having sold the other half to an investor in 2022.

The benefits of working with a financial advisor

Vicky sees a financial advisor as someone who provides peace of mind as much as anything: "It feels like so many people are after your money. Having used financial advisors, I know that my money is safe and working hard for me."

Vicky likes how a financial advisor assesses her attitude to risk, presenting appropriate options for her and her husband. Using an advisor is not just about peace of mind. Vicky is busy: "I don't have time to research and manage a portfolio myself."

She provides another example of how working with a financial advisor can produce beneficial results. "We bought our current house as a forever home. We had wanted to add a new kitchen and an extension but weren't sure how to fund it. Diane gave us some great advice. Mortgage rates were low at the time. She showed us it was more cost-effective to borrow more on the mortgage than to take out a separate loan and use some of our savings. She was right, and we had a house that was a godsend when lockdown arrived."

Vicky's current financial status

Financial security and independence have been lifelong objectives for Vicky. The couple could pay off a large chunk of their mortgage using some of the funds released from the business divestment. They have had critical illness cover and life insurance in place for years, assisted by their financial advisor.

They are also forward-thinking. Wills and lasting powers of attorney were drawn up when the children were born. As the children approach coming of age, Vicky and her husband are in the process of rewriting the wills.

With healthy savings, having paid off a large proportion of her mortgage, and a clear path to retiring at 60, Vicky is well on the way to achieving both her personal and financial goals.

Longer-term goals

When asked when she saw herself retiring, Vicky said, "I'll work until 60 but no older. I want to enjoy my retirement." Now 47, she sees having another 13 years to accumulate a large pension pot as a benefit: "I'm lucky; I absolutely love what I do. Working to 60 will allow me a larger pension, meaning I'll have a better retirement." Her husband may seek to wind down a couple of years earlier, but they are already on a path to achieving their goal.

Disposing of 50 per cent of their business has created an exit strategy. They will eventually sell more equity, but Vicky is happy to "keep my hand in" for now. She is emphatic that when she stops, that will be it. "When I go, I will go, and then we'll travel."

Throughout this book, I advocate saving from a young age. Vicky is a perfect example of someone who has done that. She is already in a great position. There is plenty of time left to increase her savings, which should provide a wonderful retirement. Meanwhile, she has plenty of capacity to enjoy life today.

HOW A FINANCIAL ADVISOR CAN HELP YOU LIVE THE LIFE YOU WANT

Frances's story

Our next example follows Frances through her life as a lawyer; she now works in eight-week blocks, allowing her to travel and do the things she loves. Once again, she has achieved this by working with a financial advisor and starting to save in her 20s.

Frances is a private client lawyer who, at 54, has made a massive life change. After over 30 years of practising, Frances has decided to stop working full time. Today, she works for eight weeks at a time, then takes eight weeks off.

Frances can only do this because she sought financial advice 25 years ago. She set up a pension, ISAs, critical illness and life cover. Consequently, she can live the life she wants in her mid-50s rather than waiting to retire ten years later.

Getting financial advice

Twenty-five years ago, Frances was a young lawyer who had seen clients struggling financially. She knew the right advice was vital to ensure her finances were secure for the future. "Diane was really good at helping me understand my options. As a woman, she made it very clear I should be financially independent, not reliant on my partner. She organised the right pensions and ISAs and emphasised the importance of critical illness cover and life insurance."

Frances says taking financial advice and putting the right financial products in place was "buying peace of mind".

Making the change

A lawyer's work is intense and time-consuming. While Covid saw many furloughed, Frances continued at the same pace. She found that clients became increasingly less patient, and sometimes received unnecessarily aggressive emails from the most vocal.

The extreme workload, and the challenges she faced with impatient clients, left Frances feeling exhausted, believing there was more to life. Several years ago, she watched a Ted Talk by designer Stefan Sagmeister entitled "The Power of Time Off". A pioneer, Sagmeister decided his practice's designs were becoming stale. Personally, he needed re-energising. His solution: to take one year off every seven. And not just him, but his whole team. Frances found this illuminating. While she did not want to follow the same pattern, she was attracted to the idea of regular breaks.

Having reviewed her finances, she realised her proposed work pattern would halve her salary. Therefore, she would need to use savings to live this new life. The good news was she had started saving so early. "Yes, I'm dipping into savings, but I have an excellent pension because I have been investing throughout my working life. Thankfully, I don't need to touch that and won't for several years."

Living a new lifestyle

Frances started her first eight-week break in June 2023. She and her husband have bought a campervan, travelling to Scotland and parts of Europe. These eight-week leisure cycles allow Frances to recharge and do the things she has always wanted to do. "I am 54. I could have worked full time for another ten years, but that just means sitting at a desk for another ten years. Having eight weeks off allows us to plan short breaks, longer trips and to do things we would never get time for." She is understandably grateful that she listened to advice all those years ago and started saving. It has provided options that she would otherwise not have had.

Frances's advice for young women

Living a life full of adventure and enjoyment leaves Frances clear about what every woman should do: "Create financial independence early. Diane drummed it into me. Save regularly, get financial protection and ensure you have a will and LPAs. In doing so, I can now reduce my working hours by half and live the life I want. And if the worst happens, and I split from my husband or he dies, I am not left vulnerable."

Taking on a financial advisor is also essential. "Diane has always been robust in her opinions. I like that. She is very passionate about women being in financial control. Her help has ensured I am financially secure. I don't have to act on everything she says, but her opinions matter." Frances says, "find the right advisor. Ask questions and assess if they have a personality that matches yours. Whatever you do, get financial advice and start saving early."

HOW SOUND FINANCIAL MANAGEMENT HELPS DEAL WITH LIFE'S CHALLENGES

Heather's story

The following example describes a highly successful businesswoman who has always used a financial advisor and been prudent with her money. Yet her life was hugely disrupted when she contracted breast cancer. Thankfully she had critical illness cover, and she survived.

Heather radiates positivity. As the Group Property & Franchise Director at the Co-op, Heather is a personable and down-to-earth woman. She gets on with stuff without fuss.

But her life has not been without serious challenges. Fifteen years ago, she was diagnosed with breast cancer. After successful treatment, she developed secondary breast cancer in 2015.

Her story perfectly illustrates how financial protection can make all the difference in how sufferers can focus on recovery and get their lives back on track.

Heather's background

Heather and her younger sister grew up in a hard-working family where money was tight. She remembers: "My dad believed in investing in property, so we lived in a big house but did not have a lot of disposable income!" Her mum was an occupational therapist, and the influence of a grandfather who was a bank manager was helpful.

Heather learnt from a young age that if you wanted something, you had to save for it. She got a TV and record player for her room by working hard at a local bakery at weekends and in the school holidays. When she went to university, her strong work ethic meant she got a part-time job caring for a girl with learning difficulties. Heather understood that earning and saving were crucial to success.

Getting good financial advice

Heather and her now husband sought financial advice 25 years ago while still in their 20s. A mutual friend introduced her to Diane, who has looked after her financial concerns ever since. An accountant for Asda at the time, she had been working for five years and had already been part of company pension schemes.

Diane provided advice on their pension contributions, general savings and critical illness cover.

Every time they got pay rises, Diane got them to put a proportion into savings.

But deep down Heather was unsure if it was worth having critical illness. She felt it was potentially a waste of money. Her view was that she had a level of income protection through work, and nobody in her family had had cancer or any other serious illness that stopped them from working.

However, taking out this policy proved to be the best decision she ever made.

Critical illness claims

In 2008, aged 38, Heather received the devastating news of a diagnosis of breast cancer. She was off work from March as she undertook a gruelling round of chemotherapy.

Diane sorted out the critical illness policy as soon as she found out. Very quickly, Heather had received her payout.

"I took out the cover to ensure we could pay off our mortgage if I got very sick. As it turned out, that's what happened, and sure enough, I paid off the mortgage," said Heather.

It made all the difference in her fight against cancer. "I was under no pressure. I was on full pay from work, and the mortgage had gone. It meant I could focus on getting through my treatment and getting better without financial stress." Not only did the payout give her peace of mind during her treatment, but it also allowed Heather and her husband to extend and develop the house in a way they could not have afforded had they still had the mortgage.

She is eternally grateful. "I know some people who have had to return to work while having chemo because of their financial pressures. Believe me, chemo is absolutely brutal. You lose your hair and feel exhausted. Not only are you suffering physically, but you also have emotional and mental challenges, feeling like everyone is staring at you. The difference the critical illness cover made was incredible."

The cancer returns

Heather had risen to director level at Asda by 2015 and was due to move to the USA to take a property role within Walmart. But cancer had other plans. She found out she had contracted secondary breast cancer. By now, she had neither critical illness nor income protection, given her medical history, but she had no mortgage and was fully supported by her employer.

However, it prevented her family from taking the USA post that year as once again she had to take several months off work to go through a tough treatment programme and get well again.

The impact from the original critical illness payout was still felt. Heather had less pressure because she had no mortgage to worry about. Once again, she could focus on her recovery rather than worrying about keeping everything together financially.

As she came through once again, she did get to move to the USA, working in Arkansas from 2016 to 2021.

She now has targeted chemotherapy every three weeks which thankfully is a far less invasive form of treatment and can go about her life normally.

Heather's financial status today

Interestingly, despite Heather's life-threatening illness, she and her husband only drew up a will just before they left for the USA. She is sensible enough to realise that she needs to revisit it, with both children now being over 18. As Diane had always encouraged her to put additional contributions into her pension, she had reached the maximum limit and could add no more. But the change to allowances in 2023 meant Heather could contribute to her pension again. Her husband also has a workplace pension, so they are well set for retirement.

Future plans

Heather is 54 and, despite her ongoing cancer treatment, enjoys life to the full. She is very active, enjoys Pilates, travelling, walking and spending time with family and friends.

Her daughter has completed two years at university, which Heather has completely funded. "I don't want either of my kids to leave university with loads of debt. That's why I paid for her course and rent and gave her a monthly allowance. She still works during the holidays and saves money for the term ahead."

Once both children have completed their further education, Heather is ready to give up work, spend more time with her husband, and have more time for herself. She has already set up lifetime ISAs for both children to help their future. Having experienced the bumps in the road that can hit anybody at any time, she is well prepared to enjoy the next phase of her life.

Heather's advice to young women

The first thing Heather says categorically is: "Start saving as soon as you can. Please don't wait until you feel you can afford it. Even if you save just a bit, get into the habit of saving money and seeing it build up." She believes in having little pots of money, those you don't touch and those you can use for a rainy day or discretionary spending.

She tells the story of life in her first job after buying her first car. "It was a knackered old thing. It broke down regularly. Ultimately, I had to pay about £400 to get it fixed. I didn't have it, so my only solution was to take out a credit card and pay with that."

Lots of people end up putting emergency spending on credit cards. But Heather makes the point that had she put enough into a savings pot, she would not have needed the card or to pay the interest she incurred.

She believes in getting on the property ladder as early as possible: "We bought that first house in our 20s. It was good for me to get into that discipline of paying a mortgage and bills. But the one thing I would say to anyone is don't put yourself under too much financial pressure."

She is a true convert regarding financial protection these days: "I had a friend who got cancer and thankfully had independent income protection. She gave up work and the policy paid out until its expiry date, nine years later. It made such a difference and gave her that choice to stop working."

Heather is a fine example of someone who has not let cancer get in the way of living a full life and having a highly successful career.

But as an initial critical illness sceptic, she has shown how being open to someone's advice can make all the difference.

One in seven women are diagnosed with breast cancer every year. Cancer Research UK reports that over 180,000 women get cancer every year. Hopefully, it will never happen to you. But for your peace of mind, ensure you have financial protection, just in case.

Your Personal Finance Top 10 Checklist

We have already discussed what you need to provide an advisor to help them review your financial position. However, if you want to be truly in control of your finances, here are the top 10 things you should continually monitor to maintain good financial health.

☐ **What pensions do you have?** What contributions does your employer add as standard? How much more can you contribute? Does your employer match your contributions? The more clearly you understand your employer's pension scheme, the better you can manage your contributions.

☐ **Do you have death in service cover as part of your benefits package?** If so, how many multiples of your salary does it pay?

☐ **If you were off sick for a period of time, how long would you be able to receive full pay?** At that point, would you receive statutory sick pay, or a reduced income through the company?

☐ **Do you have separated savings accounts for emergency spend, aspirational spending and longer-term investment?** If not, how quickly could you accumulate savings to cover these three areas?

☐ **Is private health insurance provided by your employer?** If so, do you know what it does and does not cover? Are previous conditions covered?

☐ **Are benefits like pensions, cars and healthcare available through salary sacrifice?** If so, you should calculate how much this could save you every month. It may provide additional funds for saving you didn't know you had.

☐ **Identify how much money you spend on luxury items every month.** My definition of luxury items has nothing to do with expensive watches, fast cars or designer clothes. I would advise you to calculate how much you spend on coffees, lunches, subscriptions and other spending that could not be deemed necessities. Reducing those amounts will allow you to save more.

☐ **Calculate your current level of debt.** This includes credit cards, loans and your mortgage. How much interest are you paying every month? Could you consolidate your debt to reduce interest payments?

☐ **How much do you pay for utilities, phones, house and car insurance?** Can you reduce your expenditure by finding better deals? Remember, insurers can auto-renew your policies. They have to email or write to you beforehand, so look out for those communications. You can often find a better deal elsewhere. Do you need a phone on a contract, or can you convert to sim-only?

☐ **Stay up to date about financial news.** Changes in pensions, savings and insurance regulations could impact your portfolio. You should know what those changes are and how they affect you.

Final Words

I hope that this book has been a journey of absorbing financial knowledge which has left you feeling empowered.

By reading all the stories of the incredible women who were brave enough to share their experiences, I hope you can feel a real sense of the boundless potential that lies within each woman to shape her financial destiny.

Remember, your financial well-being is not just a goal to attain, but a path to liberation and self-discovery.

As you move forward, embrace the knowledge you've gained and the tools you've acquired. Let them be your allies in navigating the complex landscape of money and investing. Your financial journey is a testament to your strength, resilience and determination.

Forge ahead, and let your choices echo through generations. The legacy you create is not just about wealth, but about the impact you make on your life, your loved ones and the world around you.

Embrace the power within you, embrace your financial journey and go forth to create a life that radiates confidence, abundance and purpose.

Your financial empowerment is the key to unlocking all the opportunities life has to offer.
We can all prosper.
Here's to your continued success, fulfilment and unending growth.

With heartfelt encouragement,
Diane Watson
She Can Prosper

Resources for Building Your Financial Knowledge

Websites

MoneySavingExpert - one of the original and most helpful sites available. It was launched by financial guru Martin Lewis to provide unbiased advice and help consumers secure the best deals in the market in every financial area. You can get weekly money saving tips, and all sorts of information to help you navigate financial products, energy costs, mobile phone providers, travel companies and much more.

The Money Charity - for over 25 years, The Money Charity has been helping people of all ages to manage their money well and increase their financial wellbeing. Their website has lots of financial information and resources, and access to free webinars and courses.

Money Helper - a site provided by the UK Government's Money & Pensions service, Money Helper is a fantastic resource for those looking to find out more about pensions and savings; there are helpful calculators allowing you to set monthly budgets, calculate mortgage payments and more. You can get help to manage your debt and, being a government agency, there are helplines if you want to talk to someone about your questions or concerns.

Clever Girl Finance - whilst this is an American site, the helpful tips to spend less and save more are equally relevant for UK readers. Such articles as How to Budget as a Couple, Do I Need a Financial Advisor: Here's How to Decide, and 10 of the Best Budget Templates and Tools, work for anyone looking to take financial control, no matter where they are.

Money Magpie - produced by financial journalist Jasmine Birtles, this is a brilliant website for getting helpful tips to save money, while getting a clear take on current financial issues. A good example is "Inflation falls to 7.9%: Here are the investments that do well when inflation is high". She is continually publicising retailer special offers and freebies and has plenty of clear information about investing and making money.

Debt Camel - a brilliant website for those struggling to manage their monthly bills and get out of debt.

Finance Girl - written by financial blogger Julie Cheung, this site covers everything from savings and investments to shopping, going green and being a student. There are many useful articles and resources on the site and Julie is generous in pointing readers to other resources that could help in their journey to financial success.

Money Nuggets - targeted firmly at women, this site covers everything from savings and investments to style and beauty and managing your home on a budget.

Books

Rewire for Wealth: Three Steps Any Woman Can Take to Program Her Brain for Financial Success - Barbara Huson

Huson was married to a man who handled all the finances in her house. He was a stockbroker who proved to follow disastrous strategies. It landed them with a $1m tax bill. Her husband fled the country and she was left having to "grow up financially" very fast.

Huson utilises neuroscience, psychology and mind-training techniques combined with original research that includes more than 20 years of financial expertise. The book will provide you with a structured process to change your approach to money and build your own wealth.

Your Money or Your Life: 9 Steps to Transforming Your Relationship with Money and Achieving Financial Independence. Fully Revised and Updated - Vicki Robin and Joe Dominguez

A great book to help you gain control of your money. It provides help with getting out of debt, how to live well for less, resolving conflicts between values and lifestyles and much more. It is a must-read for any woman looking to achieve financial independence.

Unbiased Investor - Coreen Sol

This book is aimed squarely at those who want to invest more and get better at doing it. It demonstrates how human biases can lead you to poor decisions, and how you can overcome them to create financial success.

Spend Well, Live Rich - Michelle Singletary

Michelle has created the Seven Money Mantras to help people take control of their finances. These include such things as "cash is better than credit", "priorities lead to prosperity", and "is this a need or a want?". That should give you an idea of the tone of the book, but it really provides in simple but clearly laid out terms how to control spending and better use what money you have.

How to Save £10,000 on a Low Income - Annette Galloway

Here is a book that focuses on your mindset and offers practical tips to help you save more money than you ever have before. It has only 101 pages, so is easy to digest in a day, and gives you a set of actions you can implement to help you on your financial journey.

Money Lessons: How to Manage Your Finances to Get the Life You Want - Lisa Conway-Hughes

Written by a financial advisor, this book provides practical tips to help you save more, spend less and set goals that will help you live a happy and fulfilling life.

Clever Girl Finance: Ditch Debt, Save Money and Build Real Wealth - Bola Sokunbi

This book is written by the founder of the website listed above. It too has plenty of help to get your mindset right and focus on spending less and saving more. If you've visited the website, you'll know that Bola's approach is down-to-earth and gets right to the heart of many women's issues.

Get a Financial Life: Personal Finance in Your Twenties and Thirties – Beth Kobliner

A book targeted squarely at younger women and how they manage the issues that face them during their 20s and 30s. Whether it's dealing with student debt, getting a mortgage or saving for your children's future, the book lays out a clear path to achieving your financial goals and, in many instances, is easy to implement.

Podcasts

The Wallet - hosted by Emilie Bellet, this podcast is aimed firmly at women. It covers such recent series as "Road to Wealth", and other episodes like "The Extra Cost of Being a Woman" and "Understanding the Basics of Investing with Michelle Pearce-Burke" will really help you deal with big financial questions.

It's Not About the Money - Catherine Morgan's podcast supports women toward financial independence. It has a focus on female entrepreneurs, helping them grow their businesses and strengthen their mindset. Recent episodes have included "How to Build Wealth When Your Partner Buries His Head in the Sand" and "Mastering the Art of Charging More Money".

The Financial Independence Podcast - presented by the Mad Fientist, this podcast talks to personal finance experts about their journey to financial independence. There is a wealth of information about investing, entrepreneurship, property and managing your tax.

Money Box - here is the BBC's personal finance podcast, presented by finance editor, Paul Lewis. It has plenty of advice about pensions and savings, but also provides practical tips to save for a holiday or where to go for the best credit card deals.

Clever About Cash - this is BBC Radio Scotland's podcast about money and is aimed squarely at women. Presented by Kim McAllister and Eileen Adamson, there are excellent episodes covering setting financial goals in search of happiness, how to plan your best life in retirement, activities on a budget during school holidays, and food shopping for less.

Money Clinic with Claer Barrett - the FT's podcast is hosted by financial expert Claer Barrett. You will find both entertaining and essential information in episodes including "The Financial Advice We'd Give to Barbie", "What Should I Do With My Cash Savings", and "Hacking Your Bills".

Support Organisations

We have listed a number of charities and organisations that can help you throughout this book. Do check what is available in your area.

Smart Works is a charity that supports women across the UK and has centres in London, Birmingham, Leeds, Greater Manchester, Newcastle, Reading and Scotland.

If you are currently receiving support from the Jobcentres, a women's refuge or an organisation or charity supporting women into work, ask them to refer you to Smart Works (www.smartworks.org.uk). Since 2013 they have supported thousands of women to see their true potential and are there to inspire and empower all women who need help getting into work.

About the Author

Diane Watson: Financial Advisor and Founder of "She Can Prosper"

Diane Watson is an award-winning distinguished financial advisor, entrepreneur and the passionate founder of "She Can Prosper". With an unshakable belief in empowering women to achieve financial independence, Diane has dedicated her career to guiding individuals towards a secure and prosperous future.

With almost three decades of experience in the financial industry, Diane has become a trusted voice in wealth management and financial planning. Her expertise spans a wide range of financial disciplines, including investment strategies, retirement planning, income protection and estate planning. Diane's personalised approach to financial advice has helped countless clients navigate complex financial landscapes with confidence.

Driven by her commitment to bridge the gender gap in financial literacy and empowerment, Diane founded "She Can Prosper". This groundbreaking initiative aims to provide women of all backgrounds with the knowledge, tools and support they need to take control of their financial destinies. Through workshops, mentorship programmes and online resources, Diane is fostering a community where women can openly discuss financial matters, ask questions and learn from each other's experiences.

Diane's impact extends beyond her professional achievements. Her advocacy for gender equality in finance has earned her recognition as a thought leader and a role model. She has been featured in numerous publications, podcasts and speaking engagements, where she shares her insights on the importance of financial education and independence.

Milton Keynes UK
Ingram Content Group UK Ltd.
UKHW020750141123
432548UK00016B/869